SINGLETUDE

by

Yolanda Nelson

Thank you to my mother Ruth Copes (I miss you mommy) for telling me I can do whatever I put my mind to, to my children Yockiem, Yockia, Eric, Aziyah and Sara for loving me unconditionally. To my Pastor John Suggs for holding me accountable!!!

FOREWORD

I actually changed this forward a few times because I was simply unsure about what perspective to take. I wanted to adequately and truly express how I felt about the concept of Singletude. I'm a bit of a processer so it's easy for me to start off thinking about this subject through the lens of how much God loves the "single" person, and all the time they can devote to the things of Christ.

Then you think about all of the lessons, seminars and books that suggest things like, "Just wait, your spouse is right around the corner!" Only to find out 10-years later, you're still waiting and thinking like OMG – "around the corner" clearly must have been a dead-end!

I'm so very proud of Yolanda for sharing her insight and stories about Singletude! I've watched her relive, revise and reinvent herself as a result of writing this book! I marvel at her undaunted pursuit to encourage others through her many lessons learned along the journey! She embodies Proverbs 31, not because of "title rights," but because she has committed to living out those words daily!

I think what you will ultimately capture in the words to follow is Yolanda's message about what Singletude is all about! It's not about living victoriously single – it includes that theme, but that's not the main message! It's not about taking purity pledges and vowing never to think about sex as a single, and truthfully, this book isn't even exclusively for singles!

The essence of this book is simple – "Enjoy the Now!" Singletude captures a lesson that I have been coming to grips with for a while, which is enjoying and staying in the moment. Singletude isn't about getting to a destination (i.e. dating, marriage or having children etc.), it's about enjoying the "process" of getting to those destinations and becoming all that God has called you to become along the way! Singletude is about discovering wholeness in life and fathoming how much our Heavenly Father loves us – mistakes, teachable moments, curiosity and all!

It doesn't matter if you're single, widowed, married or confused – Singletude is about enjoying the precious moments of your life and the road to "becoming…" Singletude is about understanding how every lesson you learn gets you one step closer to your end goals and dreams. Finally, Singletude is all about YOU!

You may be reading this saying, well, "I'm not looking for love," and I'm saying back, that's exactly right! You're not looking for love; however, Singletude is about love, God's love, looking for you! And, when you capture the wisdom in that statement, you capture everything needed to enjoy Singletude!

In closing, I pray that the words on the pages to follow give you permission to experience God's best for your life in the areas of love, fulfillment and wholeness! I present to you Singletude!
– John Suggs

SINGLETUDE

THE ATTITUDE OF BEING SAVED AND SINGLE

In the morning before you get out of bed the bible instructs us to put on the whole armor of God.

After you have done that you should get your Singletude in order: (See Confession)

> You are whole
>
> You are perfect
>
> You are destined for greatness
>
> All that you desire is and has been placed on the path that God has placed before you
>
> You can DEFINITELY do this
>
> It is Attainable
>
> Now you are ready to start your day!!!!!!!

Upon rededicating myself to the lord and wanting to live a life pleasing to God, I realized that there was much to learn and much to do. I was saved and single but what exactly did that mean. Well I know the first thoughts besides abstinence, forgiveness and love that came to mind was FORNICATION!

I really wanted to please God and I knew sex without being married was prohibited. That is when everything started to hit the fan. I needed help fast. I had to seek out people, places and things that could help. I was traveling down a road to which I was pretty much clueless.

The only thing I really knew was that my goal was to please God. That is what started my long journey to Singletude, putting on the attitude of being saved and single in today's society! Let's begin and I will tell you all about it.

CONTENTS

1. Introduction
2. Singletude 101
3. My Story
4. New Life in Singleness
5. Information is the Key to Breakthrough
6. Wrong Thinking
7. To have sex or not to have sex
8. I am not built for this
9. E-Factor
10. Diamonds
11. Don't Quit
12. Laws of Singletude
13. Confession
14. Salvation
15. Repentance
16. Singletude Terms
17. Journal

INTRODUCTION

Singletude was birthed from a deep and sincere need in me to have a representation of my journey from being single to a life where, with God, I felt like I could accomplish anything. My attitude of singleness changed from a punishment to an empowerment to prosper. This book is a map of my struggles, challenges and ultimately my victory through the word of God.

The number-one thing that I am trying to convey in the book Singletude is there are many roads to living successfully single, what works for some people doesn't necessarily work for all people. This is what worked for me…..eventually. It is my hope that this would be an avenue for people who are trying to live a successfully single life after having tried other things that did not work. This book is to help them find the tools they need to live in Victory.

Secondly, that they would seek out all that this stage in their life has to offer. I notice most single people look at their present state of singleness as something that is negative. It is not! It is only a phase in our life that like every other phase we have to learn to maximize our potential during the process. Your life is only as good as you make it and you don't get a do over after it's done.

When starting on this journey I knew I had to seek out information that could help me. I found lots of good material and received a lot of information but none spoke directly to some of the things that I was going through. I needed more! I needed a blueprint on how the inner structure would conform to this new way of life. I needed the processes that have to take place before you will become successful. I remember being told to "Pray about it, and it all will work out fine!"

Well in the beginning it didn't work out fine. I am not saying prayer does not work, it really does. But how could I pray if I didn't know exactly for what I should be praying. What is prayer if you don't have a basis for understanding the scripture you are trying to believe? What is it if you don't have the tools you need to have a proper corresponding action with that scripture? What is it if you don't have a strong core of what it really means to live Christian and single? Then what are you praying? Basically you are praying in ignorance and it is probably a cry for help not a confident decree that "I am whole" or that I believe when the scripture says, "I am more than a conqueror in every area of my life through Christ Jesus. You can't possibly believe that you are confident and wonderfully complete… Or maybe it was just me.

Whatever the case it is where I was then, I needed something to help me make the changes. I would have to go through during Singletude 101. I believe the difference between being unsuccessful and successful at anything is learning the basics before you begin.

It is my hope that Singletude will provide you with everything you need to help you, and others, going through the issues I will spell out in this book and find an avenue, a way out. It will help you to turn some things around and start prospering in not only this area but every area of their life. If you're current situation is not working for you and you want to try something different this is what I have to offer.

I will walk along side of you through this book encouraging you every step of the way. Consider me your personal cheerleader. Each time you confess over your life at the end of the chapter, I am shaking purple and gold pom-poms for you. By the way the colors signify royalty which is what Christ calls us, "...you are a chosen people, a royal priesthood, a holy nation, God's special possession that you may declare the praises of him who called you out of darkness into his wonderful light." (1Peter 2:9)

SINGLETUDE 101

The very existence of this book is to help build confidence, to show you that you are capable of dealing with being saved, single and living a life of Singletude. However, it just does not speak to singleness. It is to help with whatever issue you're dealing with and want to come out of victoriously. There is true victory in whatever state you are in, as long as you do not allow fear to stop you from trying something new and trusting God.

In life we have to exude a correct attitude. You currently are displaying an attitude of some kind. The attitude you display is a direct reflection of who you are and what you are going through. Instead of you displaying an attitude of desperate-tude, lonely-tude, lost-ti-tude, fake-a-tude, or the biggie Victim-tude Try Singletude!

A person's attitude represents how they feel or their state of mind about something. For example, one can have a good attitude about themselves, usually meaning that they feel good about the route there life has taken. Some people feel poorly about themselves, which affects their attitude. Singletude represents how good you should feel about the state of singleness you are in. You are exclaiming that I am Single and it is good! Don't worry if for you it doesn't feel good right now. It is my prayer that upon completing this book you will have successfully accomplished Singletude. A mindset where you're Singletude can take you anywhere you want and more.

Say to yourself right now, "my life will never be the same," One more time like you mean it! "My life will never be the same in Jesus name!" Let us begin…..

MY STORY

The wages of sin is death in other words….My Story. It's not unlike many others I came to God broken and in sin. He washed me clean and made me whole and new. If only it stopped there! I could say, "close the book I'm finished! That's it, I am NEW!" My spirit was renewed but my mind was exactly the same as before, nowhere near the saved mindset I was supposed to have acquired.

I was always in church as a child. If the doors of the church were unlocked we were there. We spent so much time at church I almost felt like it was our second home. On the choir, usher board, and any other board you name it we were there. We call them ministries now but it's the same thing. My mom instilled in her eleven children at a very young age to have the fear of the Lord. Which was really great, but in the words of Roberta Flack, "Where is the Love?" What about the love of God!

Growing up I decided soon as I get my chance I would blow this joint and I wouldn't go to church anymore. And I did! I got married at 18 and moved out and was playing grown up. At the time I really believed I knew everything I needed to know and even God couldn't tell me anything. I was grown and this religion thing was for the birds. I was ready to exercise my authority as an adult and make some big girl decisions and church wasn't in the program. There were just too many things to do. Who really wants to hear the Pastor talking about how bad all the things you like to do are and how you are going to Hell because of it. Nope, I'll pass on church. I was enjoying going to the club getting my drink on. I remember thinking while getting my party on, "Yeah imma pass on the church thing because it would just bring me down."

Unfortunately, when you are accustomed to doing something for a long time, like going to church, it is hard to completely walk away. So I decided to give church a try again out of habit and routine. That's what you did on Sunday mornings and a part of me felt this inner need to be in God's presence whether I fully paid attention or not. It was something inside that thirsted for the word of God.

While in search of a church that I felt comfortable in I was invited to attend New Comfort. A non-denominational church in South Philadelphia whose tag was something about dreams and destinies being fulfilled. Ok, the real reason I went was because my sister said the Pastor was cute and he could sing really well. I figured if anything he would be good to look at and I could get a good song out of the service. To my surprise it was little David Gaines not a little boy now but a Pastor. I always knew he would be a Pastor or something. He seemed very into God even in elementary school where I first met him. He genuinely cared for people even though he was bad like the other boys. It turned out he could sing and he was handsome and his wife was beautiful. They made a cute couple and I thought in my head, "go David she is beautiful!"

I knew there was something different about this church from the first time I stepped my foot in the door. The lady at the door greeted me like she knew me, I kept thinking all the way to my seat where do I know that lady from, it was bothering me that I could not remember her. I found out later the reason I could not remember her was because I didn't know her she was just genuinely warm and inviting and was glad that I had decided to come to the church. Wow that was big! I was used to the evil usher with the stern face and strong pointer finger that pointed you to where you had to sit.

Besides knowing David from elementary school meeting some of the nicest people I had ever met in a church the real reason I decided to join the church was because I really understood what the Pastor was saying. This was big! Up until this point all I knew of God was taught to me by my mom or the Pastor because I never read the bible for myself. Oh I knew all the scriptures you teach children. But other than that trying to read the bible to me was like reading Chinese or a foreign language. What exactly was it talking about? I still wasn't reading my bible at home but at least I could understand while I was in church. I was glad he didn't do that thing some of the Pastors did when they preached and would start breathing hard and hollering. I think some call it hooping. It always seemed like they would burst a blood vessel or something. It's funny, they never did!

I was learning so much in this church about the Love of God. It blew my mind when I understood that He wasn't mad at us rather madly in love with us. One more thing that took it over the top for me was that the Pastor would give life application. You mean this stuff is applicable to my life? They showed how I could use what I learned now while I am living out my life. It wasn't just the usual instructions on how to get to heaven that I was accustomed. This was really big to me and one of the reasons I kept going back. It was no longer routine someone had made it plain enough for me to understand the word of God!

While in church one day I clearly heard from God concerning what I was destined to do. I wasn't even clear on what hearing from God meant but I knew that He had spoken to me. He showed me who I was in him. No, I didn't hear this audible voice and the whole room didn't stand still and a bright light didn't shine from the ceiling. No, none of that. I really can't tell you how it worked but it was a conversation inside me directly to me. Wow, I was shocked God really talked to me. Nice! He told me and showed me that I was destined to do great things in the name of the Lord. At first I was tripping because I am hearing God and he's telling me all this stuff, I was super amped! Whoo hoo I heard from God yeah boy! Then it hits me…..That would mean I have to change…..Nah!

God that's alright I think I'll pass I am not there. I realized right then and there that it also meant a greater level of responsibility. That meant my lifestyle, which was far from perfect had to change. I wasn't even trying to live right at that time I was just gathering information for the future if I decided to do the Christian thing. There were things in my life that I just wasn't ready to let go. I was enjoying my life exactly the way it was. I just was not ready to say, "YES" to God, not yet. I always knew I had to do what he said even though I didn't want to. So I decided that I could do it after I finished enjoying my life a little more. I mean come on, isn't that what old age is for qualifying for Heaven.

Come on God I accepted you, let me get used to you and this Christian thing and then we can think about my Destiny later. I didn't sign up for this living my life for him, I only went to church because it was what you did on Sundays I was fulfilling my end of the week requirement. I didn't think it was fair for God to start changing the rules so early in the game.

I think the worst thing I did was choose a church where the people actually preached from the bible and they believed it. Furthermore, they taught you how to get a better understanding of God's word. How dare them! They really taught the word of God see that's where this hearing and knowing it was His voice stuff came from! I mean not that fluffy stuff that makes you feel good works on your emotions and does nothing to help you change. I think I was set up!

They even expected you to read the bible for yourself and pray and confess over your life. Exactly what was I supposed to say? It felt weird. Whoa slow yourself Christian people, pump the breaks, I am the Sunday ritual person here back up with the life changing stuff I mean who do they think I am a Christian for real! Oh it got worse…..many Sundays it seemed like the sermons were geared toward exactly what I was going through. There had to be a video camera at my house and they could see and hear my life. Then the Pastor would gather the video and preach from the Yolanda house script in the pulpit. Many Sundays I needed a drink after church just to deal with all the information that I was getting. I got a drink sometimes two it was the only way I could try to not deal with it. Change was inevitable how could I remain the same in a church where I was surrounded by so much TRUTH. Uuuuuuuuuuugh!!!! Calgon take me away, somebody help me!!!! Please, my excuses were deteriorating at that time and it caused me to change even if I was changing reluctantly. I would like to take this time to Thank God for Grace.

One thing about when God shows you who you are in Him and what He wants from your life and you decide to live outside of his will. It can be a very dangerous place to be, well for me it was that is when all H. E. double hockey sticks began to break loose in my life. Hold on tight I will give the details in the next chapter New Life in Singleness….the stuffs about to hit the fan.

NEW LIFE IN SINGLENESS

Therefore, if anyone is in Christ, the new creation has come,
the old has gone, the new is here!
(2 Corinthians 5:17)

My spirit was brand new but everything else remained the same. I still was as mean as I was before I was saved. I still cursed and would beat down anyone that pissed me off. I was still the same in so many ways. I continued the relationship I had and continued sleeping with him on a regular basis. I just wasn't there yet. (Does this sound familiar?) The only difference now is I felt this pressing urge to want to do better, to really want to please God, but how and where do you start when you're not ready to give up old stuff? What do you do when you can't or won't let go of the old you?

I wanted Christ to the point that it would not change anything in my life. I wanted him as my fling on the side in other words.... Jesus was my Hoe. He could give me all I needed without the pressures of expectation or commitment. I could visit him when I wanted and then go back home to the life style I am not willing to leave. Oh I would promise God that I was going to leave my old life and really mean it. Then get home and put on the old me. I treated

Christ and his Salvation like some of us allow people to treat them. Listen to their cheap lies and promises but because the time with them is so satisfying we continue to lead them on. God on the other hand is not man so you know what happened next!

I went to the doctor because I wasn't feeling well a little sluggish just not my normal self. I thought maybe I needed some iron or something but I was totally unprepared for what the nurse who took the routine test was about to say…..

The nurse walked in with a big smile on her face and said Congratulations your pregnant. What the HELL!!!!!!! I looked at her in total disbelief, and responded in a low serious monotone voice that made her step back. What the hell you just say to me? I asked her. I told you I was mean and she was about to catch my wrath. Surely, something has got to be wrong with your test or with you if you think I believe that! Furthermore what makes you think you should be congratulating me about it. I used several choice words that I think I will leave out.

Based on my actions I had brought about some consequences that I had to work through. Pregnant! Oh no you need to do the test over, there is no possible way I could be pregnant are you serious! Well the test was right and I was really pregnant. But how could it be possible I never missed a pill or never did anything that would cause my pills not to work. I could not possibly be that percent that even with the pill gets pregnant you have got to be kidding me.

The events that led up to my pregnancy should be in some type of daytime Soap. It's so crazy I have to share it. I had been using the same brand of birth Control since the birth of my son 9 years prior when they finally created the generic. So I jumped at the opportunity to pay less for my pills. Why is it they make you pay for your birth control pills but you can get an abortion for free with certain medical benefits? Generics weren't the problem the problem was the doctor called in the wrong prescription, not once but twice. I remember asking the pharmacist I thought they were a different color she said, "no they are your prescriptions." I didn't check why would I this has been my pharmacist for ever I trusted them. These new pills made me really sick so I went to the doctor because I was experiencing all kinds of side effects she told me to stop taking them and called in the correct prescription. What she failed to tell me and what I didn't realize was I needed to use an additional method of birth control until the new ones took effect since I was going from a stronger dose to a weaker one. Yeah really important information to leave out and that's how we get to the pregnancy.

Told you it was crazy only writers of soap opera can dream up this kind of stuff and yet it was my reality. Why me God? I am supposed to be your child couldn't you have helped me with this. I had so many plans I had just finished the preliminary test for the Police Department and was starting college in the fall. I don't have time for this. Most of all I really didn't want to have a baby by him or anyone else for that matter. I had things to do!

To make matters worse it was a crazy pregnancy I was in and out of the hospital weeks after I found out and ordered on bed rest. That was "NOT" going to happen I have three other children that depended on me. So the doctor and I came up with a plan to allow me to work if I adhered to his strict rules. Oh and did I say that me and the father weren't on great terms either, but I will go deeper into that later. Deep stuff Whew!

All the employees at my job helped out so much, the love they showed me during that time was great not just for my physical help but for my emotional help as well. I truly thank Elaine Dandridge and the rest of my co-workers at Gaudenzia they were my life lines and I don't think they ever really knew to what measure.

You see God is still there taking care of us even when we don't care about him. I was at a place I didn't know or have a way to get out of quickly. Never in my life had everything turned around because of one event. No new job, no school and now the goals I had set up were all changing and there was nothing I could do about it. Well I could have done something, but even in my sin and fallen state abortion wasn't an option for me. I understand that this is not everyone's reality and there is no condemnation for those who have done it, however it just could not have been mine. Although the enemy kept showing me how an abortion would be the answer to all my problems. You know with all the things I had to give up I could not allow myself to get past the point that this baby was mine also. My blood and DNA was running through its veins. It was a part of me and no matter how bad the timing was in the words of Madonna, "I'm going to keep my baby!" Even if that decision meant that I would have to raise it by myself.

This situation had brought me to a point in my life where everything I used in the past to pull me out would not work. I could not rely on my way of handling things anymore. I really had come to my end. There was nowhere else for me to go. I think the best way to describe it, is that it was like a death for me. But I was still alive. There was nothing, absolutely nothing sure I went through the motions everyday but inside I was numb, dull and lifeless. I wore the mask of everything is ok. But I was dead inside the only life I felt was from this fetus growing inside me. I knew I had to care for me so that it could make it, had that not been the case I really don't know.

Finally, when I had sank to my lowest and could not see a way out. The pains from the high risk pregnancy were taking its toll on my body and emotional issues with the baby's father and the overall feelings of helplessness consumed me. This one day I remembered hearing a sermon Pastor Dave Gaines preached, in it he said, "… some of your change won't begin until you die to your old self and come to your end this is where God can meet you. Or rather, now you are open to God because there is nothing else and you will let him in.

This was the beginning of new life in him. I remember being alone in my room and saying to God I heard that you could meet me here in this place and state that I am in presently. Where are you, I said desperately? I need you now with every piece of being I have left God. I can't go any further in my own strength. I hadn't been sleeping, I was in pain and I was pregnant for a man who left me when I told him I was pregnant. Every negative emotion had me revenge, hate, fear and defeat. Yes! I really needed God like no other time in my life. All the teachings I had received up until that point helped me to know that because of salvation I could go to my Father and call on him in my time of need. So I did!

I offered him no promises of what I would do if he helped me through this. I had nothing, I was broken with a longing, a complete need to cling to him, so I sought him with everything I had left in me that day.

For the first time since the situation started I felt a peace come over me, a peace that I had never known in my life before. It was better than any drug or sensation that I have ever experienced. I slept uninterrupted for the first time in weeks. It was the best sleep I had ever experienced, I felt like a baby laying in her Father's arms. No more pain and no more victim syndrome for me just this wonderful feeling of peace! I knew and felt the presence and peace of God and it felt good.

I was reborn that day, like the mythological Phoenix rising from its ashes and with this rebirth I felt an overwhelming desire to do what God requested of me. Only I wasn't sure exactly what I was supposed to do now. So my next prayer was, "I am here, so now what God? What do I do? I am saying yes but I am not sure exactly what that means." One of the things I realized around that time was when you ask something you will get an answer. Which over the next few months I felt like I was on an accelerated course. One of the answers to my question was for me to take ownership and responsibility for my life and realize the only person I can change is me.

One of life lessons I learned is that you can't change anyone else. There is no need to focus on what they did wrong. Look inside and see what you could have done better. The saying goes no need crying over spilled milk. Clean it up! Because that is sometimes all you can do. I am reminded of the scripture used in the beginning of this chapter, "…the old is gone, the new is here." In order to move forward I had to rehearse and believe that until it became a part of me.

In order for you to start on your path to Singletude you are going to have to take responsibility for your life. Hopefully you won't have to go through the whole dying thing before you realize it. If I could save you that experience, I want to say this you don't have to go there its over-rated and not necessary for change. Where was someone like me when I needed it? Well here I am for you!!!! I want to cut your learning curve now and steer you in the right direction. If you are not content with the way things are in your life you have to take on the responsibility of ownership for where you are. Here are a few pointers:

YOU ARE NOT A VICTOM YOU ARE VICTORIOUS!!!!!
1. Assess the situations in your life
2. Assume responsibility for your role
3. Acknowledge that you need God's help

Assess the situations in your life

Look at the situations for what they truly are, temporary. If you regroup and think it through you will find your way out. If you can't come up with the answers seek out others and be honest with your goals. Don't be the way I was and allow the situation to consume your every thought. It's not that Deep! (INTD) It wasn't until I was able to look at my situation from a Victor's point of view that the answers started to flow on how this thing would turn around. When I did what the bible said and counted it all joy. "Consider it pure joy my brother when you meet trials of various kinds." (James 1:2) I looked at what was going good in my life and reminded myself how even in this situation I was still blessed.

Assume responsibility for your role

There comes a time when you have to take the big girl pill and realize that some of the things that are happening in your life were brought on by you. I chose the man I was with and decided to maintain the relationship with a man capable of leaving me during my pregnancy. Yes I was an active participant in the game of life and my decisions brought me to this point. However, Glory to God I didn't have to stay here. I could make the decision to learn from my mistakes. I could learn from the failures of my past so I would not repeat it again. Then I could move on.

Acknowledge that I need God

It wasn't until I allowed God into my whole life that change could begin. You see change is not an action it is a person, Jesus! I told ya'll I accept him but he was only my Hoe on the side. He will not force his will on us but you will face consequences for your actions when you step out of God's will for your life. If you are not in his will then in whose are you? You need him! I did and my life has never been the same.

Okay back to me...The lessons that I had to learn weren't easy or pretty but they were necessary to move to the next level. In my head I thought I can't have sex so I guess I can give you that (is it really giving if you can't do it anyway?) I wasn't allowed to have sex because of the high risk pregnancy. I really didn't know on what else God would want me to work. Then it came to me, forgiveness. Ok, I can learn how to forgive those who hurt me. The real shocker was I had to start with forgiving myself. I wasn't sure what I was forgiving me for and it seemed a better use of time to try and forgive all those other people. No it was me, I needed to forgive myself. First for not following God sooner, second for playing the victim role, and third for just existing and not intentionally living my life with a purpose. I needed to forgive Yolanda for her decisions that led up to my present circumstance. Forgive myself for being human and ultimately forgive myself for consciously not following God.

In order to move on you are going to have to forgive your choices, motives and actions. So start right now I, (your name here) forgive myself for (whatever you need to forgive) and start the process of healing. Feels good don't it!

I am proud of you and once again I am shaking my purple and gold poms poms for you! I know we have a long way to go, nonetheless we can celebrate each milestone while we are on our way to Singletude!

It seemed that once I was receptive to this new life the channel was open I was getting all the information that I needed. I was hearing from God and getting information from my Pastor, on the radio and practically from any other resource available. Whatever the next step I was given the tools to accomplish it. I would get to work and my supervisor would give me a tape from church on forgiveness, I didn't even ask her for it. During my ride to work the Pastor on the radio would be speaking about forgiveness. In church on Sunday morning Pastor Dave would teach on the steps to forgive. That was how it was for every lesson I had to learn and I needed to learn a lot.

I would get constant information on how to do it, and it would really help me. If I choose to listen and do what the Holy Spirit said even if I didn't like it, I was continually given more ways to succeed. Since I decided to do this thing right and I was committed to my, "Yes" it was let's do it time, that was my attitude on the road to Singletude. Have a let's do it attitude and watch how God can move in your life!

Forgiveness

The greatest thing I learned about Forgiving is that it is not for the person you are forgiving. It releases you. You know what is strange about un-forgiveness? The people you refuse to forgive don't even think about the situation/event that hurt you. You're not talking to them, you're being nasty to them or planning revenge and you're not even on their mind. Most of the time they have moved on from the situation and you're the one who can't get past it. It's eating you alive from the inside causing you pain and heartache. Stop it! Forgive them! I know you are saying, "But you don't know what they did to me!" I don't care what they did. The only way to move past the hurt is to forgive. When my child's father walked out on me when I told him I was pregnant. Oh I didn't want to forgive him! There were a lot of things I wanted to do to him when he walked out on me. But in order to move past the situation I HAD to forgive him which I did! I am not saying it is going to be easy. I am saying that you can do it. You're gonna have to trust me on some things and by the end of the book you will get it OK! FORGIVE!!!!!

Remember we are doing this for you and your road to Singletude. You have a goal! Now that we have already forgiven ourselves now we are going to release the hold and power we have given others. You know what's next repeat after me, I, (your name) forgive (their name) for (whatever they did)….no you didn't deserve it but this is where we are. You can do it!

1. Start small at first till you get the hang of it, like forgiving the girl with the attitude at McDonalds.

2. Work your way up to the painful things and remember the 3 A's Assess, Accept and Acknowledge that you need God's help. For some you may need to seek a professional to help give you tools that will assist you in working through some things. It is OK!

3. Remember I am rooting (purple and gold pom poms in the air) for you along the way and you are more than capable of doing this!

INFORMATION IS THE KEY TO BREAKTHROUGH

…my people are destroyed from lack of knowledge.
Hosea 4:6

My next step in learning came in the form of classes given at my church. I jumped in and started the Foundations for Christian living. After completing the first class I immediately, started the next class, which was God's Plan for your life. Pastor Yvette Gaines was the one who taught my Foundations class, Lillian Hooks who later became my mentor taught my God's Plan. I was determined to find out all the information I could. I needed this for my survival. Information really is the key to the breakthrough!

You know the perishing thing for lack of knowledge scripture. Hosea 4:6, "my people are destroyed from lack of knowledge" Because you have rejected knowledge, I also reject you as my priests; because you have ignored the law of your God, I also will ignore your children." Well we live in an era where knowledge is available it's not in lack. What is lacking is our ability to seek and go after it. There are so many places on the internet that you can look up just about any subject or topic that you want. With the super highway of information there is no reason that we don't go after it.

Most churches offer classes in addition to Bible study where you can learn all there is and of course you have this book as a tool to use on your journey to Singletude.

The last class in the session was Discipleship. I learned so much in this class and I was grateful that Pastor Dave Gaines was the one who taught it. God loved me so much and cared enough that I would be taught by the best. To have our Senior Pastor teach Discipleship was just too awesome! Guess what? God loves you exactly the same and he will place people in your life to help you. I had so many questions that were always answered immediately. I learned how to worship and seek God! I learned the framework and all the little pieces I would need in times to come. I was being equipped for Destiny and I didn't even know it at the time. I remember while in Discipleship I felt extremely creative. I wrote poems and songs to God I sketched drawings of the pictures that came to my mind about the scriptures I was meditating on and what it meant to me. I realized that it could have only been because of all the time we were required to spend time in worship. Worshipping God for me had opened up parts in me that were dormant. I was learning how to seek God personally. It felt good. We had to journal what took place during our personal worship time and in class if we had questions Pastor Dave would help us sort through them. Prior to this class my acts of worship was praying before I went to bed, oh and if something went wrong praying that God fix it.

If I were to say to you that it was an easy transition I would be lying. It was very hard for me only because self-pride and what others thought of and about me were still big in my life. But as my relationship got stronger in God and then my prayer life got tight by being consistent and interweaving it into my life daily things got better. I really prayed throughout the day. Caring about the way others thought about me started shrinking quickly. I was beginning to care more about how God thought about me. Although I still felt upset about the way people would make statements about me, like you ain't no real Christian, or why you trying to get new you still the same sinner you were before and how this was temporary because of what I went through with the pregnancy. Oh and this was the biggest "let's see how long it takes before she reverts back to her old ways." I started getting negative feedback from Christians and sinners. Geesh cut me a break I didn't recall claiming at this time to be a Christians or screaming I got this thing all together. I am just working on me taking it one day at a time trying to figure it all out. I didn't feel like I belonged to either group, but I was not going to let those things stand between me and my walk with God on my road to Singletude.

The following is some of the information that I learned in class and what I used as

"Tools for your Journey"

Pray

Read your bible

Spend time with God

These are the foundational tools you will need to build upon. Once your foundation is strong you can build as high and wide as you want. Ask three people you respect that love and know you to give you the top three things that they think you need to work on. If they are saying the same thing then maybe they see something you don't. They usually do and in my case this was true. I remember asking a co-worker this question about myself. She had made a comment on my facial expressions so I asked her what else did she think besides that and she proceeded to tell me. In my head I wanted to tell her a few things she needed to change also. However, that wasn't the assignment so I accepted the response because basically it was true. In my spirit and mind I was changing however there was no outward expression of that change. I was still portraying an unchanged attitude. I was not at Singletude yet.

No Outward Change

Your change starts inwardly. This is a process like anything worth acquiring it will not take place immediately. If you are to be successful you have to be committed to change. There is no need telling people or screaming to the top of your lungs that you have changed, SHOW THEM! Better yet show yourself by pressing on despite the fact that no one else is aware of the new you. God is looking. And always remember I am cheering you on every step you take in the right direction towards Singletude. I have my purple and gold poms poms waving shouting from the sidelines of your life saying, "I SEE YOU, you better go ahead with your confident self!"

The Process

To encourage you I want you to know that the things I experienced did not take place overnight. Oh how I wish there was a magic wand that could be waved and it all could be redone correctly. For some of you this process to Singletude will not be as long but for others it may take a little longer. However long just know you are the only one who can control the speed of your progress. The process is exactly that, a process! It took you more than a minute to jack yourself up so trust me it will take some time to get yourself together. Just keep having a victorious mindset and continue telling yourself, "I may not be where I want to be but I am no longer where I used to be." Rejoice in your baby steps. Start a Journal to record your progress and track your development. (See journal at the back of book)

Review your mind

You have to renew your mind! "…Be transformed by the renewing of your mind." (Romans 12:2) In order to do that you have to review where your mind was before you started this journey to Singletude. You have got to be brutally honest with yourself. Find out where your thought process is and seek out the error in your thinking. Once you have done this you can begin to renew (restore, refurbish, renovate) your mind. Think of it as renovating your thought process the way you would renovate your house. You wouldn't go in and gut out the old house then start over with brand new things. This could be a costly process. First you would fix the broken things before you try to beautify the home. Why would I paint my bathroom and the toilet isn't working. Your life is the same begin to repair the broken items first and we can get to decorating later. Prayer is how you find out which problem to fix first. Allow the Holy Spirit to do its job and lead and guide you in the maintenance. "But when HE, the Spirit of truth, comes, HE will guide you into all the truth…" (John 16:13)

Learning to respond appropriately to people who hurt me thru prayer was one of the hardest lessons I learned in renewing my mind. My prayer should be for God to bless them as instructed in 1 Peter 3:9. "Do not repay evil with evil or abuse for abuse but repay with blessings, because to this you were called so that you may inherit a blessing." In the beginning I remember wanting God to be my hit man and bring down his vengeance on them for me. (It's a process!) I knew that was not how HE works and if my goal is to live this life right in the sight of God. I would need to learn this praying of blessing thing and learn it quickly. Practice, practice, practice is what I did even when I didn't want to do it. Over time it was easier for me because of repetition. Once you recognize how important everyone is to God and in order for me to let my life and actions glorify God blessing others is a must. In order to be able to handle where I was going I had to learn these things. If you are not there yet, it's okay keep reading and I pray you get there. Always remember it is a process…..

Since my relationship with God has been growing and strengthening I have never been in lack. I wake up with a smile and sleep well. If there is one thing I would like for you to receive from this chapter is, "don't believe the lies of the enemy or of those in your past." I live peaceful nothing missing nothing broken. Because of the change in my life and my devotion to Christ my children have gotten a closer relationship to God. They know the real me and they would comment on the change in my life constantly. Before Christ many of the trials and test that I had to face would have devastated me to my core. Now I know that I win and it's only a test I am going through. The trying of my faith is for the word sake and I should not take it personal. "…because you know that the testing of your faith produces perseverance. (James 1:3) I knew that the test was working a process in me and they were witness to it. Your life is not fine without Jesus! Life is beautiful WITH him and while you are in process mode learn to enjoy every step you take forward. If you find yourself taking a step backward don't sweat it, turn around and get back on your path to Singletude!!!!!

It's not until you fully accept him that you will understand the fullness that you are missing out on. One of the most devastating things for me to realize is that I took as long as I did to get to where I am. I wish I could get those years back but I can't. Take the limits off and expand your thoughts to believe only what the word says about your life. Not what you were told as a child or any derogatory statements from past relationships or the self worth you have created in your head. God sees you as, "New!"

Only believe that your Destiny could be revealed, and your dreams fulfilled and you could be living a life of good health, wealth and Joy on your way to Singletude! It's not deep!!!!!!

WRONG THINKING

> Do not conform to the pattern of this world, but be transformed by the renewing of your mind. Then you will be able to test and approve what God's will is his good, pleasing and perfect will.
> (Romans 12:2)

Sin Cycle

I would like to describe for you what I call the sin cycle. There are five parts to this cycle wrong thinking, active sin, guilt and condemnation, back sliding and lasciviousness. It is a cycle of events that once you start the cycle it leads you through a process that you might not enjoy going through. Read on as I go deeper into what this Sin cycle is.

Wrong Thinking

For as he thinketh in his heart (mind), so is he: (Pro 23:7)

Wrong thinking leads to wrong actions! Lets me start out by saying every thought you think is not necessarily yours. It is however, a seed that was placed in your mind. Somewhere in your life a seed was sown for that thought you are thinking. What I mean is at some point it got in your psyche (mind).

For example: You are driving down the road and Marvin Gaye's song "Sexual Healing" comes on the radio. I would like to believe it was his intent to describe to you the relationship of sex as he sees it as a medicine to all that ails him. Marvin Gaye said, "When I get the feeling I need Sexual Healing". So in your mind either intentionally or unintentionally you could later equate sex with some type of healing. If you were making love to his song (for those of you who have gone back to that place right now, get back to reading) you have a memory or have placed a seed in your mind. Every time you hear that song you can return to the exact time, place and for some of us feelings you experienced while listening to it. (If that is you, I am serious take control of those thoughts racing in your head right now and get back to Singletude).

Just by reading a line in this book and not really hearing the song you probably started thinking of someone you had enjoyed sexually with that song. So again I urge you to get control of your thinking and thoughts. Start to replace wrong thinking with thoughts that are pure, or right thinking." I refuse to think on that right now. That's why the bible instructs us to renew our mind, daily! "Do not be conformed to the pattern of this world, but be transformed by the renewing of your mind. Then you will be able to test and approve what God's will is his good, pleasing and perfect will." (Rom 12:2) You cannot stop a thought with a thought. You have to say something contrary to the thought otherwise it will continue."

I am saying all of this to remind you how sensitive and powerful your mind is. That is why the bible speaks of guarding your heart.

It is speaking of your mind and how you should be on guard against things that will get in it. Am I saying you should not listen to Marvin Gaye, NO! I love Marvin and as soon as my Man God created for me shows up, there will be a lot of Marvin Gaye being played after we are married.

Please guard your mind if Marvin Gaye or any song or image gets you to a point where you are dwelling on areas you are working on. Turn it off! It may possibly cause you to sin. In the earlier days to my Singletude I could not listen to anything but inspirational or Gospel music. I couldn't even play Jazz because I still remembered the words. It may not be an issue for you but if it is close some doors until you are strong enough to enjoy it.

Active Sin

For the wages of sin is death; but the gift of God is eternal life through Jesus Christ our Lord. (Rom 6:23) Let's talk about Sin and give it definition. In short sin is missing the mark. In archery the red bull's eye in the center is the mark and any place other than that red area is termed sin. In the context of this book, I really like that example because whenever you miss the mark of the Law of God you have committed sin. I am not going to go into the laws you have your own bible and most of us know them by heart already. I will go into the degrees of sin. There are NONE, I repeat NO degrees to sin. Sin is Sin!

There is no such thing as small, little, grey, white, baby,
not too bad, I only did it one time
it's not like I murdered someone sin

This sin is too great, extraordinary; I did it again after I asked God's forgiveness for it,

I was doing so well but I messed up sin,

This sin is worse because I have an important role in the church! I think you get what I am trying to say. There is no degree to sin, Sin is sin! So the best thing is to try and avoid it as best you can.

Active sin is when you have start thinking wrong and your thoughts produce an action. Like when married people who cheat on their spouses make the statement, " it just happened." No it did not just happen! I have never seen anyone walk down the street and trip and fall in bed with someone. Somewhere along the line the thought got into their head and then they began dwelling on the thoughts in their head. After all it's only thinking who could you hurt with a thought? But then their actions follow the thought. That is why I want you to start actively thinking about what your life will look like after you have achieved Singletude. Start preparing your mind now.

For example: You are driving your married self down the road and an old song like Sexual Healing comes on the radio. Then you remember an old flame and your thoughts go back to when you and the person was giving each other a serious case of sexual healing. Instead of taking control of your thoughts, reminding yourself that the person is in your past, remembering you are married now and your thoughts should be of your spouse. You get into the sexual healing of the moment. You do what is called in the bible "throw off restraint" in the area of your thoughts. In allowing yourself to be in wrong thinking you give the enemy authority to get involved.

Have you ever wondered why you started thinking about an old flame in a sexual manner or after they suddenly call you out of nowhere? Well make no mistake it is not out of the blue. It is a Penagina trap set up by the enemy to cause you to fail. A Penagina trap is a trap that you fall into when your penis or vagina start to make decisions for you. But please REMEMBER when you open the door to the enemy and give him permission to enter in he will wreak havoc on your life.

Wrong Thinking Example:

It starts out like this.

EX: Hey I was just thinking about you so I thought I would call, I hope its okay said the old flame.

You: *Sure it's okay, matter of fact it's funny you called I was just thinking about you.*

EX: Oh really what were you thinking about.

You: *Well our song was playing on the radio and I remembered some of the things we used to do while listening to it.*

Ex: Wow! That is ironic because I have to admit that I was listening to the same song on the radio and could not help but call you.

That is something alright it's called a Penagina trap. What are the odds you both were listening and thinking the same thing? After you talk further finally the subject of your spouse comes up and instead of you informing the person of how happy you are. "Wrong thinking" has you considering how good you and Mr./Mrs. Sexual healing would be in bed. How good it was and you start to compare them with your spouse.

It sure is funny that you can't really remember why you broke up. Only all the good sex and fun you two shared. You may not act on it right then but you have just sown some seeds of infidelity. By not dealing with the situation correctly you are on your way to Active Sin. Active sin is where you are actively and knowingly are participating in sin. Please don't lie to yourself and believe that you were just talking to them. Your intent is strictly personal and you have just started a cycle of sin in motion.

Right Thinking Example:

Your response after you answer the phone should go something like this:

You: "It is nice to know that you were thinking about me I hope all is well.

EX: All is well says the old flame.

You: You may not know it, but I am married now. God had truly blessed me with a wonderful person who loves me. Communication is the key to many marriages surviving the test of time. One of the things we discussed was how to react to old friends now that we are married. I cannot wait to tell my spouse that I talked to you. I think it best that you do not contact me anymore but it was really good hearing from you.

You have just let them know that you are married and you're going to tell your spouse you spoke with them. You are informing them that you are serious about your spouse and you don't keep secrets from them. You have also made it clear that you are happy with your spouse and there is no room for them. They will remain in your past.

Since this is a book about Singletude, let's put it in the context of being single. Let them know the same thing you are secure and confident in your new life and you plan to leave old things in the past. There are several major reasons why you call them OLD or EX! Leave them along with your old thinking and other things you have Ex-ed out of your life. Congratulate yourself that you did not get caught up in active sin with Mr. Ex.

You might be thinking to yourself what is wrong with having conversations with an old flame or your Ex-mate? Well for one thing, the manner in which this particular scenario started. It was not a pure one, it was created out of a sinful thought. Remember Wrong Thinking leads to Active Sin and the cycle begins. Singletude is here to help you stay off the crazy roller coaster that says it will be different this time.

If sin is what is driving the discussion, then everything is wrong with having a conversation with them. Especially if you have sexual thoughts you are trying to get into control. You cannot allow your temporary emotions brought on by the Penagina traps that will come to distract you from completing your goal to Singletude. Be prepared ahead of time by knowing what you are going to do and say and stay on guard so you will not fall prey. This works in any area that you dealing with be it _____, (put whatever you are dealing with on the line) whatever thoughts get you started into active sin.

Guilt & Condemnation

Therefore, there is now no condemnation to those who are in Christ Jesus... (Rom 8:1) What are your thoughts of something being condemned? Is it no longer good or worthy? I am sure you can think of a few for yourself. Your wrong thinking caused you to take part in an action of active sin and now after the sin comes condemnation, guilt and fear. At this point if you have a relationship with God you usually pull away from him because of what you have done. After you engage in active sin you experience guilt, like when you cheat on your spouse, curse out a co-worker or lie on your taxes. The feeling immediately afterwards, or sometimes during that make you feel unworthy is a feeling of guilt it tells you that you are not good enough to be in God's presence. WRONG THINKING! This is when you should be running into the presence of God. Repenting for what you have done (see chapter on repentance) and receiving his forgiveness. Remember Romans 8:1. 'There is therefore now no condemnation to them which are in Christ Jesus who walk not after the flesh, but after the Spirit God can and will forgive your action." Yes that action you did when you _____ (fill in the blank) he can forgive that one too. You may be thinking he cannot possibly forgive the time you _____ (fill in the blank) YES that one also. He can and will forgive your sins once you repent.

As far as the east is from the west, so far hath he removed our transgressions from us. (Psalms 103:12)

Does the fact that God will forgive you of your sins give you permission to sin knowing he will forgive you. No it is not a get out of sin free pass.

I like to note that you never needed a pass when you were in active sin. You did it because it is what you wanted to. The cheating spouse did not trip and fall into infidelity they planned it. You did not make a mistake on your taxes when you asked your cousin could you use her child as a dependent you planned it. You didn't accidently curse your co-worker out you rehearsed what you were going to say including every finger and head motion. You did all those things without asking for permission. You wanted to do it and you did it!

The problem is we don't forgive or forget what we have done. There are consequences for your actions. This is where we allow the enemy in by not running into the presence of God for forgiveness. We stay in our active sin which leads to the next step backsliding. You probably thought you got away with the sin because no one found out about it. You and your partner in crime know. Now you are feeling guilty and afraid that your secret will be discovered. You have also opened the door to the effects of the sin. We know the payment of sin is death. When you start this process it's like putting in a job application for Sin and now every day you are working diligently for your check of death.

It does not have to be a physical death. It could be relational or the biggie spiritual death. There are a lot of consequences that comes with each course of active sin we participate in.

Who knows what your payment will be if you continue to stay in the sin cycle. Are you willing to pay the price for it? If you read the chapter on New Life in Singleness I told you what my payment was. And guess what it also had negative effects on my immediate family and other relatives who I didn't even realize were paying attention to my life. People you don't even suspect are watching you! The co-worker who silently listens as you talk of how God is blessing you. Your neighbors who watch you as you come and go to church. The person who travels on the train with you wonders why you can be so happy. Your family and friends are watching you waiting to see if you are sincere. They want to see the Jesus in you. What are you showing them?

Back Sliding

But when the judge died, the people returned to ways even more corrupt than those of their ancestors, following other gods and serving and worshiping them. They refused to give up their evil practices and stubborn ways. (Jud 2:19)

Backsliding is the term used for going backwards. So instead of moving forward like you were before you got onto the sin cycle you are going in reverse. You are not standing still like you may think, you are actually going backwards. You are getting into things that you overcame in the past. Now because of the guilt and wrong thinking you slide deeper and further away from God you're trying to drown out the voice that reminds you over and over again that you are missing the mark.

In Judges 2:19 the children of Egypt were fine while they had a judge over them, but when the judge died they picked up their old habits and a few new ones. They were now more corrupt than before. Sounds a little familiar, you probably said to yourself you would never cheat on your spouse (or curse your co-worker out, lie on your taxes, etc.).

Here you are doing the one thing you said you would not and enjoying it. I said I would never inflict the kind of pain on any one that my husband inflicted on me by committing adultery. I was devastated over him cheating on me and destroying our family. When I was on the sin cycle I did the very thing I vowed never to do to a person who loved me. I cheated on my then long-term boyfriend. I am very aware of the sin cycle and how it works.

While things were continually getting stressful at home instead of doing the right thing I decided to stay away from home even more. In my mind I knew I was the source of the tension and I did nothing to solve it. It was all about me then. I was enjoying what I was doing and now I was a fully-fledged back slider. I was dedicated to this thing. Oh SIN feels good, let's be truthful It felt really good to me. But how good is it when the consequences start to hit? Is it really that good? Was it really worth the sequence of events that followed? Was it worth hurting the person you love? If I could go back to the beginning and do it all over, I would. I would handle it totally different than I did. But I can't change the pass. Neither can you. Backsliding can cause us to do and be people that when the smoke clears even we don't like the person staring back at us on the other side of the mirror.

Lasciviousness

Meaning: lewd, provoking/exciting lust; given to/or expressing lust; immoral, lustful, lewdness,

This is the last level on the sin cycle. Lasciviousness means basically you are now being driven by lust and your preoccupied with you own lustful desires. I like when my Pastor says, "…you cannot drive into your future looking out your rear view window." In this case you are driving 120 miles forward and looking out your rear view window and you are about to have an accident for sure. You are so deep into your lascivious behavior that you fail to think about your family and how this is affecting them. You are selfish and just thinking of your desire. You are right where Satan wants you. In active sin and stuck in the Sin Cycle.

I have said it before and will say it again, the true result of the sin cycle are negative consequences. Consequences are the effect, result or outcome of something that occurred earlier. Now your spouse is about to leave you, you've lost your family. Relatives are wondering what is going on because they assumed all was well with you. Now the facts are coming out and they really want to know what was going on in your mind. How could you mess up your life? I could go on and on about some consequences and I am sure you can think of a few of your own. Maybe your consequences have not caught up with you, so think of someone you know. To put it plainly, what is done in the dark will surely come to the light. Well when the light starts to shine are you ready for what you and everyone else will see? I don't think you can even imagine how Satan will use this for his perverted scheme to get you out of discovering your destiny. Oh you may have opened the door a little but the enemy has a way of sticking a door stopper in it so he can come and go as he pleases to wreak havoc on your life. You let him in!

NOW, it's time to kick him out! How do you do that after all the things you have done? I am so glad you asked. Just repent (see repentance) the bible speaks of how God will make everything work out for your good. Remember God never intended some things for your life and I would think you cheating on your spouse would be one of those things. God holds marriage as sacred. He is so awesome that he can turn that situation around or whatever caused you to get into the Sin Cycle. God will work it out.

Repentance will put you in right standing; however, it will not magically correct the situation. God will still allow you to go through the consequences you have set in motion. Yet, there is forgiveness and healing that can take place while going through. Remember God will be there for you to see you through it!

The key to defeating the Sin Cycle is to not get entwined in it from the beginning. Control your thoughts which produce actions. I have given you a scenario of how it could get started but there are many roads to the Sin Cycle. Remember the battle is not yours it's the Lords, but there are real things you must do to stay off or get off the Sin Cycle. You have to avoid the following.

Here they are:

1. Wrong Thinking – Control your thoughts and keep them pure and of good nature. If you find your mind is going into places that you are working on find a person to be accountable to. Usually the person that tells you like it is not what you want to hear. Listen to them and get your thinking in check.

2. Active Sin – Whatever your sin or sins are STOP! Repent and follow step 1 and start to renew your mind through the word of God. If this is you I want you to know that you can do it!

3. Feeling Guilty or fearful – Remember this is where the enemy attacks you and tries to tell you that you are worthless or a bad person. DON'T BELIEVE THE LIES and get back to step one. God loves you and is not focused on your shortcomings he is more focused on your righteousness.

4. Backsliding – Turn around and start going forward by following steps for 1-3. Run to the presence of God. You are worthy and he loves you, YES YOU!

5. Lasciviousness – Just remember this is the danger zone where you think you don't know how to stop. Well just stop right here and now, remember the sooner you repent and get

back to going forward the better for you. You can do it, I am here with my purple and gold pom poms rooting for you. Get off the Sin cycle for good and start living the good life that is out there for us. It does exist for you. Reach up and GRAB IT!

TO HAVE SEX OR NOT TO HAVE SEX

It is God's will that you should be sanctified:
that you should avoid sexual immorality
I Thessalonians 4:3

Dreams and destiny consume me, so it's easy to forget about sex. My standards have changed and meeting a man with my required qualifications is not very easy or at the top of my list of things to do. I wake up enjoying and loving my life exactly the way it is, sex is that last thing on my mind. But what happens when Mr. Right comes across my path and he meets all of the requirements. What happens if we both have chemistry and he is or at least seems to be good enough?

This chapter is a way for me to explain that while it may be easy to abstain from sex when there isn't an offer. You know out of sight out of mind. You can feel courageous and triumphant that you have abstained. What I am saying is do not allow it to be a false sense of security. You cannot shop if you don't have money. You cannot over eat when there isn't any food. You cannot drink as long as you are not at the bar. What will you do if you find yourself in a situation where you have to make the right decision? In your journey to Singletude you will be faced with the question, "To have sex or not to have sex." The bible says, "It is God's will that you should be sanctified: that you should avoid sexual immorality." (I Thess 4:3) It is very clear that we should avoid sexual immorality. But trust me as I write these words there will come a time when you will have to ask yourself the question should I have sex or not.

We are up against a defeated but clever foe and the experiences of our past can cause us to remember things that have no place on our path to Singletude. So as I give you tips and pointers on how to keep yourself holy and acceptable to God, I want to let you know there will come a time that you will have to make a choice.

Your wrong choice can put everything that you are currently working on at stake. Your emotions will feel so powerful and overwhelming that it might feel if you don't give in and have sex you will fail to exist. Trust me it is a trick of the enemy. You can make the right choice if you want to!

The challenge is to get rid of the old life "style" of our past. You will have to put off the old way of doing things. To realize in order to get something new you have to try something new. That process takes a while and can only be accomplished by changing the way you think and react. God has already written a new code for your reprogramming. It's His word. All you must do is read it, accept it, and live it. Please read on as I tell you a story of a woman I will call Whattodo, who had to decide to do things either the wrong or correct way. Hold tight as we proceed through the process of making the right or wrong decision to have sex.

Today is the first date Whattodo will have been on in years. She is excited because it is with an old friend, Mr. Cocoa Brown. She really liked from the first time she met him, but for reason beyond both their control they didn't pursue anything in their past. When they ran into each other again they exchanged numbers. Wow, who would have thought after so many years they would both still feel the same way? So many decisions to make, where does Whattodo start in this new playing field? She is not sure if she knows all the rules. She has changed a lot since the first time they met. In the past her standards were a lot different than they are now. Sure she knew what not to do, but what exactly is OK? She decided to be herself and enjoy the company and stop stressing over the unknown.

Since he never told her where they were going Whattodo didn't know how exactly how to dress so jeans cute top and heels was her choice for the night. This way she was ready for most places. She put on her face, hair was fierce and she was ready! He was late! He called and explained that he would be. He finally arrives and there he is so fine and sexy, Mr. Cocoa Brown with a fresh cut and that million dollar smile that caught her eye in the first place. He is exactly what she desires in a man and of course she is thanking God for him being there for her right now.

Whattodo loves a confident man that can dress and loves God…to what degree she cannot really be sure of yet. But boy was she really interested in finding out more about him. He is and has been active in his church for many years. So far so good he seemed worthy enough to spend some time with and get to know more about.

As they continue the night talking she was amazed at the attraction she has for this guy. Where did that come from," Whattodo asks herself. The overpowering she feels for him takes her by surprise. She has not been on a date in a while. Not because no one has asked, no one she had met till this point has moved her enough to make the extra effort it would take to go. There have been some very sexy men but no depth. The ones with depth usually were from a different religion and she didn't believe in wasting her time. Sometimes it was the preliminary check on them that would come back unacceptable. If you don't know what this is make a note, the preliminary check is when you do a serious check on the potential person. It is very important that you do your research on men before you allow them in your company, especially a police report! Hey it's there why not use it to your advantage. You can Google someone's name and they pop right up good or bad. When you know who you are and where you are going you don't have time to waste. Whattodo didn't have access to his records but she hit the street trying to find anyone who knew him and anything about him. She would ask friends who may be in the same circle and she checked all social media. Mr. Cocoa Brown passed all the checks with flying colors and was worthy of her time.

When you start to enjoy your road to Singletude like Whattodo, you start having a crazy busy, beautiful and fulfilled life and allowing someone into it requires making changes. She was not willing to compromise on this part at all. Ok, so let's get back to Whattodo's date night. So they were off in his car, which was clean and neat, to go bowling. First impressions mean a lot and he was doing good so far. "So, I was thinking, he says in his deep voice, we could shoot some pool," Whattodo raised her eyebrow at him, "Why did you say that?" she said. He looked at her and smiled his teeth almost shimmering in the car. Then he gave the sexist look with his beautiful brown eyes and well groomed moustache and thin beard. Did he just lick his lips? Whattodo smiled in spite of herself. "Well," he continues in his deep voice. (Did I say his voice seems to caress her with every word?) "Well, you said it when I texted you." He faces her for a minute, "What you didn't think I was paying attention?" He does a little chuckle, licks his lips (AGAIN! DANG IT!!) and turns back to continue driving. Sure enough in her text she had put it in there she wanted to play pool. He asked via text the things she liked to do and she texted him several things that she would like to do on their date. Whattodo didn't know how to play pool but she was willing to learn. He actually paid attention to what she said. She is really starting to feel this guy right about now. He's sexy and HE PAYS ATTENTION TO THE DETAILS.

    They get to the bowling alley and he starts to gets out of the car, of course Whattodo stays seated. He looks back and says with a smile "I don't open doors for women." She says, " it's ok, I'll just be here when you get back." And she meant it! It doesn't really matter if he was joking or not Whattodo was serious and she knows something you have to teach people how you want to be treated. She knew he was joking because he had the umm umm umm smile when he said it. But he did work his way to her door! Wow, this guy is sexy, he pays attention and knows how to treat a lady, and she was enjoying herself already. Whattodo is having a great time and wondering why she stopped dating in the first place.

Inside the pool hall he places himself behind her, wrapping his muscular arms around hers and placing his hands gently upon her hands, to show her how to properly hold a pool stick. She is taken aback and totally caught off guard by the smell of his cologne. It smells so good, a verbena-citrus scent and she can feel emotions stirring up each time he comes near her. It's electric! She is somewhat intoxicated by him. Everything about this guy is right on target. He is doing a great job of teaching her to play pool. He was encouraging even when she didn't hit the ball and instructive on how she could hit it. He kept telling her she could do it with an added umm umm umm smile. His actions were very caring and patient. She enjoyed learning and his ability to make the experience enjoyable. He is stirring up some emotions she thought she had in check. His perfect biceps peek out to say hello each time he leans in to study his pool ball and then strike it. This man is one of God's finest creations in every way, created perfectly sculpted and defined with exquisite detail from head to toe.

Whattodo is having a wonderful time and so into the game, she kicks off her heels. They laughed out loud and it seems he is enjoying the company as well. Pool is fun and being there with him makes her feel so comfortable, like she belonged in his arms.

Guess what? She was finally getting the swing of the game, but before she can enjoy her new found success, he changes the game. He increases the difficulty, by giving her a terribly hard shot to maneuver. Whattodo looks at him with her well made up "Are you serious?" face. He responds in a smooth reassuring tone "You can do it!" It was a bank shot into the corner pocket past a ball that was in the way. YES I can, she exclaimed, she positions herself and delivers much to her surprise. She made the shot! She really didn't think it would go in but she gave it her best and it worked! She is as excited as a little kid who just learned how to shoot a 3 pointer. You would think she had just won the game with how happy Whattodo is with Mr. Cocoa Brown. And he is just as happy that she made it as her! Caught up in Mr. Cocoa Brown's umm umm umm smile and glistening pearly whites. She actually leans into the celebratory kiss he offers. Once their lips meet she melts in his arms. His lips were soft and the aroma of his cologne along with the feel of his strong arms around her is indescribable. It's as though time stood still and no one else in the place existed. She couldn't even hear the sounds of the place that surrounded them. As his lips begin to explore hers she feels a warm sensation come over her that completely engulfed her. It feels so right she didn't want the moment to end! When their lips finally part she watches him as he gazes at her confidently. (She didn't know what to say, but she sure was screaming in a good way on the inside).

After what seems like an eternity she steps away from him. She feels a little dizzy and asks herself what just happened here? Her intentions were to give him the celebratory peck on the lips how did she end up searching for the ground beneath her so she wouldn't fall? She was really weak at the knees at this point, so she holds onto pool table for balance. You may say to yourself that it was because she hadn't kissed anybody in a while so it was bound to be really good. You need to know she has never kissed anyone in her life like that kiss. She has never felt the emotion rage through her body like that before. It was as if he was created just for her. She wanted to feel that again immediately, and over and over again. It was more than sexual it was intimate, sensuous and caring. Kissing him in that moment felt like something he had wanted to do for a long time. Now that he had his chance, he was going to giving it his all and WHEW did he ever!

They go back to the game but all the shots she makes after that are really off. He promises to kiss her again if she makes another shot. And you know she really wants him to do it. So she tries even harder with the skills he taught her to make another good shot. She wants to be back in his arms feeling his lips exploring hers, his arms wrapped around her, reliving the safety and sensuality of being back in his arms. However, Whattodo's knees are still shaking too much from the first kiss to sink another ball! I guess either sensing her irritation at not doing a good job or wanting to help so he could kiss her again he suggested he help her. As he walked closer to her, all the nerves began to come alive before he evens touched her. In anticipation of being close to him again the excitement is overwhelming and building she is a little scared and pleased. His hand reaches out and pulls her close to him, with the strength and care he gave as before he guided her with the way it should be done and the shot was strong and powerful, she made it! Soon as the ball rolled into the pocket, she could feel his hand around her waist guiding her closer to him. Those lips awaiting hers this time she knew what was about to happen and eagerly received him. This time she was prepared to react, she wrapped her hand around his neck and with the other embraced his chest softly as he pulled her close to him. This time, Whattodo was prepared to answer the exploration of her lips, teasingly, pleasingly, tasting him and relishing him giving back all the passion that she had received the first time they kissed. Oh, she was ready and he knew it, yes he was the giver but she had experience on how to receive and wanted him to know it.

I know you are thinking, oh, girl please, it was just a kiss. But if you have ever felt your eyes roll back and the tension melt from your body, you know exactly what she felt in that moment. It was so crazy she wanted to laugh out loud afterwards; it was that good. She didn't think he understand exactly what it meant and her head was still too much in a fog to explain. Her emotions were all over the place. Like being scared on a roller coaster ride, you can't stop laughing hysterically. She wasn't sure why it was she wanted to laugh all she knew is this is the stuff romance books are written about and it was only a kiss, Wow!

They finished their game and sat down to talk. This was the opportunity to ask the questions to get to know Mr. Cocoa Brown. So she started asking questions like......How many kids do you have, are you dating other people, what are your plans for your life. She needed something to help clear the fog and shake her back to reality.

They continued to talk and enjoy each other's company. She realized the more they talked that Mr. Cocoa Brown was a great guy. Then he popped the big question. He asked, would she like to go to his house and watch a movie with him? Hell yeah, is what she was screaming in her head; let's get outta here right now. I'll race you to the car. It's only a movie no harm done. You're both adults and you could probably get some more of those sweet, succulent kisses. Her emotions were screaming, YES!

She respectfully declined and told him thanks for asking and they talked some more. He explained how he was celibate for over three years at one time. She knew that meant he wasn't anymore. She commended him on his commitment to getting close to God and honoring him with his body. She also asked if it is difficult being a man and celibate. He explained, the first two years was ok but the third year he met someone. They started out fine just talking a little on the phone, then the conversations turned explicit, heavy petting started and you know how the story ends. Mr. Cocoa brown and lady friend had sex, Whattodo had been in that situation before, so she just listened.

Then of course, he asked how many years had she been celibate, and she responded that it had been five plus years. She didn't think exacts mattered at this point. He commended her on being faithful in that area they continued to talk as he drove her home.

They arrived at her house and he asked her again, if she would like to go over to his house to watch movies. She smiled and declined again. His response was that she would be safe with him. Whattodo wasn't scared of Mr. Cocoa Brown, she had no doubt he would honor her, "No" if she wanted him to stop. The problem was could she even articulate the word, "No" or would she even attempt to stop his advances. How could she spend time alone with Mr. Cocoa Brown when she felt such a strong attraction to him. She knew he would be like Heroin to a new user; once you try it you are addicted! It would be like leaving a steak in a tiger's cage and not expecting him to eat it. He was not the problem. Her emotions were and they were alive and in living color. She was warm and flush with parts of her body trying to take control over the situation. They started screaming to her, Pa leeeeeeeeeeeeaaaaaaaaaase GO with him, Go with him now! It's only a movie! What harm is there in a movie and a little kissing? Whattodo started thinking to herself how much could she get away with Mr. Cocoa Brown and still remain saved.

She chuckled to silence the noise her emotions clamoring in her head and body. She kept telling herself that she didn't wait this long to give up her celibacy just because her emotions had been awakened. She didn't stop trusting that God would give her the desires of her heart. She had to remind herself that she was in control of her body and not lose confidence in her Singletude. She didn't need to help God by going over his house and giving into temporary fulfillment. Thank God, her word was strong but her trust in the Lord was stronger.

Temptations are all around us; it is our job to recognize it when it rears its ugly head. Or sometimes it's very handsome Cocoa Brown head. We have to make the right decision, one that we will not regret later. You know how I know this? Because Whattodo is really me. Yes I was the one on the date. I 'm not gonna say my triumph felt good at that moment. Every fiber of my being screamed and begged for him to satisfy what he just awakened in me. I wanted him to answer its call and I'm sure he would have been perfect in his response. It did not feel good at all but I decided it had to end before I changed my mind. Before I gave up the confidence I had built over the years, and before I lose my Singletude card and all my privileges revoked. Most importantly before I allow my emotions to cause me to experience a disconnect between me and Jesus.

I know you may be saying, girl that is why you repent. Yes, there is repentance. I was giving myself the same excuse to allow him to pleasure me. Oh I mean, "while we were watching a movies." But what about missing out on what God has for me? Because thoughts are like an addict wondering and focusing on when can I get my next fix of Mr. Cocoa Brown.

We must know our strengths and limitations in order to navigate this thing called life. In battle a good warrior knows his strengths and weaknesses. Mr. Cocoa Brown was mine. Let's be real, wasn't any movie on my mind at the moment. So the only thing for me to do was get out of the car. So I did! One of life's best lessons is to always be real with yourself. It will guide you when you are lost.

Yes I wanted him, I wanted to finish the night off with a trip to the moon. Yes I wanted to release all the passion that was inside of me with him. However, does this fit the plan? I was able to remember the plan for my life and on what I was working. I don't just want sexual fulfillment! I want and require a loving respectful relationship. The only way to get it is to learn how to make the hard decisions. I want it all! And the only way to get it is to continue to maintain who I am despite my emotion. The verse I was reminded of, "But seek ye first the kingdom of God, and his righteousness; and all these things shall be added unto you." (Matt 6:33) Even a mate that is as sensuous, strong, caring, smooth and sexy as Mr. Cocoa Brown. Yes, I trust God. In saying goodnight to him I knew it had to end. He evoked such strong emotions from me and the battle was too great. You have to learn when to back off and regroup and when not to play with FIRE!

My weakness is sex and I don't play with this thing. For you it could be something else (lying, stealing, and gossiping). I was not prepared to allow it to stand in the way of the plans for my life. I woke up the next morning very pleased that I didn't drop the ball. To tell you the honest truth it was very satisfying to me. I felt my Singletude Confidence Meter on full, now that my emotions were quiet. That night as I lay in the bed reading text from Mr. Cocoa Brown explaining how he enjoyed his evening with me; the battle that raged inside felt like I had just run a marathon. I was exhausted!

Ladies these are not just words that I write. I KNOW! I understand the things you go through. I go through them also. Probably in greater measure at times because I am the one shouting words of encouragement. "You can do it! With my Singletude bull horn blaring loudly and cheerleading pom poms shaking violently back and forth." I'm shouting. We are not animals our instincts and emotions don't drive us. We have been given the ability to make choices despite what we feel. We are in control of our emotions not the other way around. So do not allow yourself to fall into a Penagina trap. Remember it's when you allow your penis or vagina to start making decisions for you. When you see the trap, don't just stand there and accept it or fall into the trap do something about it. You are very capable of making the right choice if you really want to.

If you just want the physical fulfillment then go home with your Mr. Cocoa Brown and watch all the movies you want. But if you are like me and I believe you are, you want a relationship worth substance, the commitment along with the great sex. Not for a moment but for a lifetime. If that's you then you will have to make the strong decisions and move on.

Reward yourself for not losing the battle. Continue what you were working on before, distraction stepped in your life. There are many things you will have to do that may not be easy but they will be rewarding. Remember while on your road to Singletude you are more than capable of doing it!

Remember the Triple A's

1. Assess the situations in your life

    Ask yourself is this situation I'm in worth what you have been working hard over the past months. You will find it is not. It is a temporary problem that will go away if you allow it. You are better and bigger than your emotions. When we believe that we are not bigger than our emotions we reduce ourselves to a soda bottle. When you shake up the bottle it has no choice but to over flow. But you are more complex then soda. So when our emotions get shaken up we don't have to overflow we have the power to quiet our emotions and move past it. In order to live a life of Singletude you are going to have to get your emotions in check.

2. Assume responsibility for your role

    As long as you are single you have to protect your purity. Outside stimuli will always be present be prepared to respond. Will all your dates be the same as Mr. Cocoa Brown? Maybe or maybe not but you should always be prepared for battle. No one is above the questions of whether they should have sex or not have sex our strength needs to be in Christ, which leads us to the third A

3. Acknowledge that you need God's help

    You will have to enlist the help of the Holy Spirit. We need his super on our natural. We have to always be listening for him to lead and guide us. Beware; do not press the over rule button when we hear the Holy Spirit and choose to proceed anyway. The bible speaks of the Holy Spirit as being a comforter please allow him to do what he was created to do. It is very comforting to know you didn't make a mistake and that you are still on your road to Singletude. He knows what to do even when we don't.

I AM NOT BUILT FOR THIS

I praise you because I am fearfully and wonderfully made; your works are wonderful, I know that full well
Psalms 139:14 (NIV)

After the last chapter I know some of you are saying to yourself. "Oh I am not built for this." If that was you and Mr. Cocoa Brown you would have sealed the deal and repented for it later. You are definitely built for this and more. The bible says we were fearfully and wonderfully made. (Ps 139:14) Which means we are capable of doing exactly as, "the Bible" is instructing US? You were never meant for some of the relationships, or people you had in your life. You were built for better and greater things.

I understand that society and some people in the church have decided to give their interpretation on how things should go within a relationship. If you are TRULY going to get to Singletude you are going to have to follow the blue print set before us. The Bible is the manual for our lives and that is our only point of reference. So let's talk about what God created you for and what you were not.

What you were created for in my words....

God created Adam out of his image and gave him a company to run, the corporation called Earth. Adam had full responsibility over it. While on his job as Co-Owner/CEO of Earth. He mastered his skills and did what he was told by the majority stock holder. God saw that his choice was exceeding every goal. He wanted to reward him with a bonus worthy of his accomplishments. God who knows all and sees all knew what this hard working co-owner needed. He sent him on a vacation (sleep) and while he was vacationing he created the best gift. It was an assistant for him while he dominates the Earth. It would comfort him in ways Adam could not imagine. The assistant would accompany him while they together carried out the Mission of the corporation. The gift, God decided would be called Woman. He knew everything good that was in Adam so he pulled out of him the essence of his being and added to it all that would be needed for these two to work as one.

This woman he created had all the inner workings of Adam and more. She would be able to produce more of what God considered good, She was created to continue the line of Adam owner/CEO of the earth. (Gen 1:28) So I say to you, if God created you to dominate with Adam then why it is you would think you are not built for this? He saved the best for the last of his great creation. You are the apple of God's eye....he made Adam from the dust, but he took you out of Adam. I want to believe while Adam slept HE had uninterrupted time, without Adam telling him what he thought he wanted, to sculpt exactly what he needed. Please stop living beneath your dominating quality, your rightful royalty. HE calls you a royal priest hood and a mighty people. (I Pet:2:9-10) Contrary to what you believe you are BUILT FOR THIS! You were sculpted by the very hand of God for a wonderful and mighty purpose. He put Adam in charge of caring for this earth but he made you the replicator of him! Do you understand what I am saying God feels that you are so precious he has given you the right to recreate! He entrusted you with the future generations of the earth. This is a wonderful thing through your womb Salvation came! You are beautifully and wonderfully made. PERIOD!

Do not choose to believe the lies of the enemy or whatever you're past tells you. I urge you to speak to your past and say! "Old things are passed away and today I stand as a new creation in God." (2 Corin 5:17) Then pray:

"Father create in me daily a new person that will only believe what your words says that I am."

What you were not created for, "Abuse"

If God has given you a gift that is made to comfort and accompany you why would you abuse it? We read in the beginning of this chapter my interpretation of creation and how woman was created and given as a gift. It is said that hurt people hurt people and I am sure we all can relate with that statement in one way or another. If you find yourself in an abusive relationship and you want to believe that the person hurting you physically has brokenness from their past, I urge you to pray for them but I do not give you permission to accept the abuse. They may need professional help.

Pray they receive it maybe help them find it. But you are not a counselor or psychiatrists so please do not think it is your job to fix them. The only person you can fix is you. Your job is to comfort and accompany the Adam of your life. However, if he is not displaying Owner/CEO qualities I suggest you move on. When you accept the abuse you are supporting their brokenness. Love does not abuse. If he is hitting you LEAVE! Find out what is in you that would cause you to accept that kind of treatment and use your energy helping you.

I had a friend whose boyfriend and father of her child would beat her, and she didn't know why. She would do what he wanted her to do the way he wanted it done. She believed if she became perfect he would love her and not abuse her. No matter what she did it was never enough. She accepted the beatings, and subsequently she lost her identity and he continued to abuse her throughout the relationship. There was nothing wrong with her or her actions. It was him he was broken and nothing she did could fix his brokenness. She finally left him and moved away. Years later she still harbored hatred and disbelief as to why he treated her that way.

First I told her to forgive him, and the second thing I told her was to forgive herself. She was shocked and a little angry as to why she needed to be forgiven. As long as she continued to think of herself as a victim she would be one. She is not a victim nor was she a reflection of her past situation. She was a recipient of a bad situation, however, the moment she decided to change it she became a victor. Forgiving him released her from his mental control.

Forgiving herself, made way for Victory! She could celebrate her strength, not waving the flag of her past defeat. She could start fresh as a whole person not a victim.

You can be victorious after leaving a past relationship of abuse, but you have to heal from your past before starting a new relationship. Take time out to reevaluate what you could have done differently. Remember: We cannot change other people, we can only change ourselves. That means asking the big girl questions…such as why did I stay, why was it ok for me to accept the abuse? What is it in me that I need to work on so that I won't allow the abuse again? How do I stop the past hurt from leaking over into my new healthy relationships?

When you take the time to heal and forgive yourself, you open up to the possibility of a healthy relationship and most of all a healthy you.

Victim syndrome

It is a person's willingness to accept whatever has happened to them because you are the victim and have no control over the situation. I know he says he will never ever do it again, but he has shown you that he will. I have heard the saying. When someone tells or shows you who they are….BELIEVE THEM! His words say he will not do it again, but his actions show you that he will. His actions are consistent and trustworthy, you should believe them. This is not a fairy tale! This is your life and you do not get a second chance to try life again. Once you are dead there is no way to push the restart button. There is a separate dialog between people who are victims and those who live victorious.

Victim: If I do whatever he wants, the right way, next time I won't bring punishment on myself.

Victor: I am worthy and too valuable to allow someone to hurt me physically, emotionally or verbally. I deserve better.

Victim: He was mad, I should not have said anything to him until he calmed down and was in a better mood.

Victor: I have a right to speak and be heard, if he can't respect my voice or agree to disagree than he cannot have me.

Victory begins when you believe that there is a way that you can make the best out of your life and it starts by not allowing yourself to accept that you have no control over IT! You have to change your thinking in order to change your life. The way you change your thinking is to believe who God says you are and rehearse a new script.

SINGLETUDE CONFESSION
(a new script)

Father God, I decree and declare that my single life will glorify you. I receive you as Lord over my body, spirit and soul. I will seek you first in all that I do. I pray that your will fulfill its purpose in my life.

Father God I confess that every financial need is met and that I will not lack or want for anything, In the Name of Jesus. I speak with power and authority that my life is prosperous.

I bind up every generational curse, strongman and stronghold sent against me. I loose the Spirit of Truth, Love, Joy, Peace and Liberty over my Singleness,

In my singleness I will walk in excellence, Love, Character and Integrity at all times. I will Pray, Fast and do what the word of God says for my life to accomplish what God has set it forth to do with diligence. I place a demand on myself to walk in obedience and submission.

I choose to live a holy life pleasing until God and the lust of my flesh has no power over me. I am committed to be diligent in the things of God. I will spend quality time helping to advance the Kingdom of God,

I thank you in advance for what is going to take place through my life. I receive that it is in your word that when I first Seek the kingdom of God and all its righteousness all things that God has intended for my life shall be added unto me.

Satan you are defeated, I am more than a conqueror in Christ Jesus, and no weapon that is formed against me will prosper. In the name of Jesus I release every ministering Angel assigned to my life to go forth and cause this confession to come to pass.

In Jesus Name Amen.

Put good words and thoughts in your mind and good words and thoughts will have to ooze out. If you start to do these things consistently you will start moving in the direction of Victory in every area of your life and your road to Singletude will come quickly.

What you are built for

As I sat back one day I thought about how God sees us as his children and more importantly his daughters this poem came to mind I pray it encourages you on your road to Singletude.

Your head has been crowned with spirit of his wisdom and grace, your shoulders were created to give strength and range of motion. Your arms help to uplift and strengthen your mate from the worries of the world and help to protect and carry life that has been created inside you. Your breast warms his head at night and gives life to your offspring. Your womb is a place of warmth and reception of his imprint of life and the sustainer for the next generation. Your hips were created to support your womb while new life is growing inside of it. It helps the body to receive him as he explores the innermost of your being as you become one. Your thighs keep your body sturdy and flexible while allowing you to maneuver the concern you both will encounter in this life. Your knees remind you that there will be times of bending and the best place when that happens is to be on them in prayer. Our calves help us raise our heels and lift up those situations in our life that try to bring us down, also it allows us the strength to lift up the people who are in our life. Our ankles help us to support the weight of the responsibility that

God has placed inside of us he has entrusted this to woman. Our feet integrate the rest of this wonderful body it absorbs the shock and takes on the load of the family and places it beneath them so they can proceed forward.

This is what you were built for and the next time you feel that an event that is beneath your perfect design is overwhelming or you can't handle it. Remember the strength that God has placed inside of you and say to yourself, "I am built to withstand anything; I can do this because I was built to overcome any obstacle!"

You were built to comfort and accompany the owner of the earth. If you own something you know about the inner workings of that thing. You care for it and treat it with love and kindness. If someone feels like you are a part of the company. They will respect your assistance and enjoy the comfort that you bring. Yes! You were built exactly for this.

THE E-FACTOR

He who finds a wife finds what is good
and receives favor from the Lord.
Proverbs 18:22

Did you ever meet someone and say to yourself oh he's just not my type there is something about him that I really don't like. I am not talking about major issues, just maybe he's not cute enough, doesn't have the right job or maybe he doesn't share your beliefs. He doesn't have all that you require in a relationship. We will call him Mr. Right Now. So on first impression you write him off. You are clear that you are not feeling him and not interested. This is not a problem for Mr. Right Now he has been imprinted with a need to conquer and is ready for the chase. Not only does this fuel his interest in you it puts him in hunter mode. Since you are off limits you have just become his prey and he will do anything and everything to finally get you.

You are clueless to what has just taken place inside of him. I believe God fashioned the picking of our mate was given to the man. His word even says that a man "finds a good wife." I am not a bible scholar but I am not versed on any passage that says the woman finds a man for her husband. So I am to believe that since it was created this way there had to be some things put in place for this to become a reality. There is something within us as women that was given at creation and passed down through our spiritual DNA. I call it the E-factor short for Eve factor. The conditions of this genetic trait are simple. We were created to receive him! Our bodies were sculpted in expectation of receipt of him. So he is the pursuer and we are the receiver of his pursuit.

Since we know he is the pursuer and we are the receiver she meets him he's not her type. He wants her and could care less how she feels. He will start his pursuit. We as women have to realize that this is something that we can't change about ourselves. However knowing is half the battle. If you know that you have this trait you have to make the decision in the beginning that you are going to receive the pursuit or shut it down. If I am not clear let me put it to you plainly so you can understand.

You meet Mr. Right Now and you don't like him, he on the other hand has already picked you and now it's on the Hunter vs. Prey game. He will increase his game to whatever level is required to get you. You are marked and he will not rest until you're bagged, you're his boo and it's game on. You are the woman he wants and he is ready and willing to move mountains to get you. You haven't even given him a second thought. Until you get the flowers on Monday morning at your job. You think it's nice and what woman doesn't want to receive flowers at work. Scenario after scenario will take place until you either shut it down or surrender to his pursuits. If he is good he will have done his homework and asked around for the things you like and then commenced to shower you with it all. You on the other hand being single accept the gifts or attention because in your head he doesn't have a chance in Hell and why not you really like the things he is buying you.

The big problem is the e-factor somewhere or somehow it will happen if you allow yourself to treat this lightly. He will get in and all the ill or negative feelings you felt will be replaced by warm feelings and before you know it the e-factor has happened. You are falling for this guy you weren't even attracted to him. It happens within the first six months and then after that no matter how hard you tried to keep him at a distance you will start to feel strongly for Mr. Right Now. Guess what? Now he is your boo and your loving the attentions. If you think I am lying think about a partner you didn't even like in the beginning and because of his intent on being with you yall finally got together. And you sit and talk to your girlfriends and say the famous lines we all (if we are honest) have said in our dating life. "I remember when I didn't even like him and now I can't get enough of him." Don't get me wrong this is not a bad thing because I believe it was given by God. It's a wonderful factor put in place to ensure that we will procreate and receive the pursuer if he pursued correctly. God is a good God and he has given all things accordingly. So I thank him for the E-factor. It should work out well he sees what he wants and goes after it and she receives him after he has proven that he is worth it.

There are only a few ways the e-factor can hurt us for instance when you find a man you don't desire to share your time or life with. Don't play! Make it known clearly and do not receive his advances. It's real easy unless he is a stalker. If that is the case then proceed to get the law involved quickly. Most men are not stalkers they are just hunters they will push the envelope and try to rise to the occasion to get you to surrender. Make it clear that you are not interested. Clear means no accepting his attention, gifts, money, flowers or advances. There are many ways you can "Shut it down." You don't have to be cute about it let him know this is not where you are trying to go. He will get the message, he is a hunter not stupid. You are really in control because you are thinking with a clear head there are no emotions attached. Make the decision and stick to it.

How this works in our favor is because his initial lack of potential in the beginning is not a barrier to us falling in love with him. I have asked a few people that had arranged marriages and they all said that they did not love their spouse in the beginning. All of them said that there came a time when they were madly in love with them and the feelings remained.

We have to be clear about what we want and if a person does not meet the bill don't waste his or your time. You will get caught in a situation asking yourself, "How did I get here?" Know what you want and what you will stand for in the beginning and if Mr. Right Now does not meet the core values then RUN! I say core values because the other things are really not important. For instance the car he drives, how he dresses, and where he works. The priors are not what I define as core values. Core values are how he treats you, is he respectful, does he share your beliefs, and does he have vision. If you want someone that shares your value systems don't compromise with the Mr. Right Now because he is after you and you love the chase. It's not worth ending up with a man that does not respect you just the hunt. Men tell you who they are in the beginning, they usually have diarrhea of the mouth and will let all their stuff come out good or bad. You have to know what you are listening for. A side note when you start to date someone his representative is the one you are dating. For that matter, your representative is there also. You don't really spend that much time and energy on getting ready on a daily basis. You speak differently and act differently in the beginning. It should not come as a shock that he is doing the same thing. Be on the lookout for when the representative slips up and the real person shows up.

Example

If you are at a restaurant and the waiter does something wrong and he flips out. The real him has shown up and anger may be something he wrestles with. Don't let it slide, put it on the table and ask questions lined up to reveal whether he deals with anger problems. You should be prepared for this and other scenarios and the questions should come out normally. Study for a date like you would study for a test.

If you are out with Mr. Right Now and you notice that every beautiful woman that walks by captivates him and he zones out for a few seconds, it could be a clear example of what you can expect during your relationship. There are many other examples but I will leave this as my last one in this section. When you discuss past relationships and the women are painted as the sole reason for the breakup, pins all the problems on the other person. Sentences like, "she just wasn't good for me" and "maybe I shouldn't wear my heart on my sleeve" come up. Thank him for dinner, offer to pay for your own meal, call a cab and leave. He is one of the many men who cannot and will not live up to their shortcomings and will always blame others. That means in the future, the problems in the relationship will be blamed on you. There are absolutely no unions where one person is at fault. It is a two person problem and his inability to see his shortcoming will be a problem. Mark my words this is a proven fact!

I dated a guy who was the full package or at least I thought he was. In the beginning he was all of the things a woman prays for. He was attentive and loved to shower me with gifts. Not to mention gorgeous! I was able to check off everything on my list of who I would say is a perfect mate. In the beginning it was subtle he would talk about his past relationship and the women. I really disliked this one chick after all he said about her. Why would she do all the things she did to him? He was so nice. Well yes he was nice but he was a male victim. He never did anything wrong and was clueless why she acted the way she did. Well long story short he was the problem he never took ownership of his actions it was always someone else's fault. So of course when we broke up it was my entire fault. The stories he said about how I treated him in the relationship were amazing. I really wouldn't like the picture he painted of me. (sound familiar) It was crazy all his friends thought I was a monster. There was a party a mutual friend had and I was asked to bar tend for her. I got into the whole scene by calling myself a bartender name and all. I met all of his friend under a false name (not intentionally) but I like to play and have fun. We all got along and had a great time. One of his friends asked our mutual friend where was the "B" that hurt Mr. Shortcoming he heard she would be at the party. She laughed because she knew the real story about our relationship because she was both our friend. She is here and she pointed to me. They said that's Francesca (I can't remember the name I gave) they responded that it couldn't be and said nah! That can't be her she is a sweetie there has to be a mistake. It wasn't! I Francesca and the "B" were the same person, me. They all realized that day that the stories didn't add up. I have to go on record saying that I was not innocent either. I was at fault in many ways, just not to the level he gave me. I can admit to my shortcomings but when the man does not have any. That is a red flag we all have issues and when you find an issue free man run in the opposite direction.

Use what God has given us to protect us from making a mistake. There were red flags and sirens going off inside of me with Mr. Shortcomings. I chose to proceed and found out no matter how much you wish your intuition was wrong you saw this coming. The E-factor is not instant so you will not fall prey to catching and falling in love with the wrong guy if you use the other great thing God has given us....YOUR BRAINS, when someone shows you or tells you who they are BELIEVE them. Ladies we have been created with the ability to love and love deeply make sure that the person you are lining up for that type of love is worth it.

DIAMONDS

She is more precious than rubies; nothing you desire
can compare with her
Proverbs 3:15

There is a phenomenon that is sweeping the nation, and soon will take over our youth. Well not really however I would like to describe this chapter like it is a real epidemic. It is of epic proportions and it does not discriminate. It crosses all lines of race, gender, age and financial status no one is immune to it... It is called FWB, Friends With Benefits. Please read closely people! There is presently no immunization that can protect us against it. The symptoms start out slow, and give the impression of a harmless and advantageous situation. But the big issue with FWB is its slow onset. It grabs you by surprise. It is not until you have been subjected to the phenomenon and enjoyed its "benefits" for a period of time that the effects start to show up. It begins to affect users almost immediately and can last for weeks. The active ingredient is consensual sexual intercourse, which is highly pleasurable and brain altering. When high doses of FWB are experienced the following four stages can be experienced.

Stage one is hallucinations- Hallucinations are things you really believe are present. This is the one symptom that is experienced immediately, since it causes one to believe that their relationship woes have been solved and that this is the best scenario ever. Women fall prey to its effects at a greater rate than males.

Stage two is delusion - you really begin to have a fixed erroneous belief that this present condition of FWB has satisfied every need that a traditional relationship could. You are sold on this deception and while the euphoria process still has you in its temporary pleasurable grip, the exaggerated physical and psychological hold is starting to reap havoc on you. You are becoming deeply immersed in the lies, and becoming a willing participant of FWB.

Stage three: The most devastating stage is impaired memory. While FWB can be notably enjoyable in its earlier stages, by the time you reach the third stage the negative side effects like temporary amnesia start to slowly take effect. Cases show that females have a higher experience with this than the males. We are not totally sure why it is uncommon for the man to feel the effects of FWB amnesia; although there are a few reported cases. The reason I believe may have something to do with the female having a higher production of the chemical estrogen. Studies are still in process. (not really this part is hypothetical) However, from what we know the female will experience this and it will continually get worse as long as she subjects herself to this situation. She will start to forget that she and the male are not really in a relationship and that she means more to him than they agreed in the beginning. She will begin to believe they are a couple; which usually causes great pain to the women in the end.

Stage Four: Disorientation - the participant forgets what position she has willingly signed up for, she has lost her direction. The woman is usually in a constant state of confusion as to her role in the relationship to the extent that she now believes that they are more than friends. It is said that the anxiety and fear of being alone is one of the common causes of this onset of disorientation. Her decision making skills have become blurred and she is at the point of addiction. Sexual satisfaction, physical stimulation, and orgasmic release that FWB has been known to produce it also causes the negative reaction of withdrawal. This can send the participant on the downward slope of the high which is enforced by the emotionless connection of the relationship. FWB has been compared to the same feelings drug addicts feel coming down off their high. It builds to a climax only to leave its participants filled with desolation and emptiness. Last effect is withdrawal, the person is left constantly trying to seek another hit of the high that FWB has been known to give.

While there really has not been any scientific studies done, to my knowledge, on this Friends with Benefits phenomenon, I wanted to explain it in a way you could understand. This is my interpretation of the stories the people who have been affected by it explained their experience to me. This is my fictitious way of getting these serious and very true effects of being in a sexual relationship with a friend.

Some of you may be saying to yourself, what is the problem with that? It seems like a winning situation especially if you would rather not be in a serious relationship. What could be wrong with this situation if it is between two consenting adults? Before you make a decision please read the following...

FWB has adverse reaction when you subject yourself to it. The very thing that could be viewed as a solution to your temporary problems becomes in itself a big problem. If you don't believe me please reread the *E-factor* chapter. Women were not designed to be involved in these types of relationships. Sure women can adapt to anything, but it will never fully satisfy them. My goal is that you be fully satisfied and not just sexified.

Whether you believe it or not you are in a type of relationship. Instead of signing up for flowers and fine dining you opted out for sex. You have just lowered your bar to the point it doesn't even exist. You have told him that he is totally acceptable to sleep with exactly the way he is. That he doesn't have to be anything in particular or provide any of the things men should provide like protection, stability or love. You have communicated to him that physical pleasure is good enough for you. Oh let me not forget the friendship. But who are we kidding here; friendship changes once sex is introduced. Bottom line; you have just made a choice to lose self-respect and a friend all for being sexified. Sexified is the term I use for a person that is ok with only being satisfied sexually.

The guys' point of view is they don't respect the girls that are just sex buddies. She says Friends with Benefits and he calls it Sex

Buddy, two totally different things. It means that you are no longer friend material either. Friends can hang out and go places, sex buddies are good for one thing......say it with me SEX!

I want to be very clear with you women who are involved in this type of relationship. Have the conversation with your male counterpart or FWB and ask the real questions. Also be prepared for the answer. Talk about your thoughts about where you guys are, trust me they will be totally different. Men seek gratification from a physical nature and women usually from an emotional and physical nature which means your feelings will always be involved where he can be totally disassociated. For him the sex is just sex. Please don't just take my word for it ask male members of your family or your friends that you don't receive benefits from. They will explain it to you in detail the same way they have explained it to me when I asked the questions. Ask about five males. I have asked more than that, but I want you to hear it firsthand. These are not my thoughts its how men think. I really want better for you and you deserve better!!!!

Women have to stop living this fantasy life in their head and be present in the real world. Now if you see it for what it is and you are Ok with the way things are going, proceed. I am speaking to those who have decided that this just ain't working for them and want to do something about it.

I explained to you in detail in this chapter my hypothesis as to why these things are not good and you will find out quickly that once women start sleeping with a man, they can try but, because of the way we are wired, they will start to have real feelings for their partner. However, on the flip side of things, men don't seem bothered by it at all. They can sleep with you and treat you like a friend for years and not feel the need to be in a serious relationship with you. This is the very reason I want you ladies to make sure you use protection against this FWB phenomenon. The only effective defense against FWB is abstinence, to not start using it in the first place. One you start you can become addicted to it and the side effects get more prominent the longer you are involved.

For the men, before you jump up and down and say to yourself, "This is great! Free sex and you don't have to do anything to get it. Where can I sign up?" Sure I can understand in the beginning it is all good. You have the best of both worlds, you get a cool female friend that is willing to give up the goods. Plus you don't have to remember her birthday, compliment her on her hair, or even ask about her day…..none of the stuff that you would be required to with a female you were dating. All you have to do is call and make sure she is available, who could ask for anything more. Well, just to let you know, even though she is your friend, in her head she is working out an unconscious plan to make the deal permanent. No she will not bring you in on this conversation. Well, at least not in the beginning. It is going on in her head. There are some women out there that buy into the FWB and some way during the relationship they believe that they can change your mind or better yet that they have control over their emotions.

There are worse things than a friend wanting the relationship to go to the next level. They make movies about the other type of women and conditions that may develop. There are stalkers and fatal attractions and you say to yourself, "Nah, not my girl! We good friends and she's not like that." True she may not be, but you won't ever know a person until you start sleeping with her. It's a different vibe. So before you go singing the praises of FWB, there are many negative side effects that come from it.

For example, you have a FWB situation so you feel pretty confident and you start dating not caring if you are going to score because you have your FWB in the background who is a sure shot. So, if things don't work out you are still covered. Problem is when FWB finds out that you are cheating....yes cheating. I know in your head your saying how could you be cheating because you two are technically not in a relationship. Like I said it's a different ball game in her head we are wired different.

Let me tell you about a case of FWB. I spoke with a group of girls about their single life and we discussed modern relationships since they were 20 + years my juniors. I wanted to get a feel for what the thoughts and feelings of the younger generation's thoughts on relationships were and the temperature that exists now. We discussed many things openly and candidly. One of the subjects we talked about was Friends with Benefits.

Benefitishia, is what we will call her, told me that she had many relationships that were FWB's. When asked why? Benefitishia said she preferred them to actual relationships because she didn't have to deal with the baggage that comes along with the traditional relationship. For example, she said they knew the rules of the friendship and they didn't expect anything from each other but sex. She spoke of it like it was a matter of fact for all people. I on the other hand, needed more clarity. This is what I got. They both did not have a partner but had sexual needs and since they were cool what would be the harm in sleeping with him.

In the beginning she and the friend were real nonchalant about it until the questions came out. What happens if either one of them wants to start to date someone. That was an issue dealt with when it happened and not discussed before hand or during the initial decision to sleep with each other. The man has no problem reminding the female of the boundaries. He will make sure the boundaries are respected and if he can't keep them in place he will usually choose to dissolve the relationship. All he signed up for was a sex buddy, not a girlfriend. If he wanted her to be his girlfriend he would have placed her in girlfriend category instead of just FWB's.

There is a distinct reason that this is your title; because he does not believe that you are fit to be his wife. Guys view women in two distinct categories which are serious and not serious. Serious category is when he gives his all to the relationship. He thinks of you and wants to do things that he believes makes you happy. He is serious and nothing will stand in his way of letting you know this. Not serious category is when he doesn't care about you or what could make you happy it's all about him. So if he is not serious about you or cares enough to respect you and claim you as his girl then you are in the other category.

I know I'm from a different generation and view things differently but WHEN is it ever ok to give up your diamonds so easily. Even before I decided I was tired of living my life the way I was, I never thought it okay to take such a precious gift and give it away so freely. Yes, I made mistakes that I wish I could go back and erase from my memory and history, but the FWB's never ever crossed my mind. There has to be a commitment to me. I am not ever going to knowingly sign up as just a sex partner. Now I know my last statement sounds judgmental but keep reading I am going somewhere.

If the women of today knew their worth, how precious their body is, and how God views them, I don't believe they would be so fast to just give it away. How do I know this you say? Because I asked Benefitisha what would she do if I gave her a handful of rare diamonds? Would she just give them away to anyone who asked? Her answer was a roaring, "NO!" She said she would not give them to anyone. She would keep these rare and expensive jewels to herself. Well Houston we have a problem, God views us as rare and of quality. He calls our bodies' temples of the Holy Spirit. I am sure he sees his temples as places of the rarest quality.

Diamonds are classified by ratings the rarer it is, the more value it is worth. That is how we as women should think of our bodies. You are special….Let me say it again…YOU ARE SPECIAL! If no one else sees you that way always remember Elohim, the King of kings calls you special. So special that he has inspired pages of whom you are in him. "She is worth far more than rubies…a woman who fears the Lord is to be praised." (Prov. 31) This is how your creator sees you as a woman of worth and value. You are not just a sex buddy.

DON'T QUIT

Quitters never win, and Winners never quit
Vince Lombardi

What is it going to take?

Sometimes there is a serious disconnect between what we want and what it really is going to take to achieve it. Everyone knows the saying, "if you want something different you have to do something different." Writing this book has been my way of showing you that this concept really works. I can write about Singletude because I experience it every day. I live in Singledom, however, it did not come without challenges….I had many but the defining factor was when I decided that I can't have something new doing old things. That was when things started to turn around for me. I want you to experience the same success.

The first major question you have to ask yourself is if you are willing to do what it takes to get what you want. If your answer is yes, please know that this is a journey. Like most trips/journeys there will be hard times but if you stick to it, it is very rewarding. I say hard not because it is impossible but because it will mean you are going to have to change the way you think. You'll have to learn new ways to deal with old situations.

Carmel and Sweetie had been in a long term relationship. They were good together and had been this way to each other for a long time. Sweetie decided she was done with the Relate Ship and she wanted to get on the Married Ship. She loved Carmel but knew that it would never work out. Carmel was a great guy and one would consider him a great catch. He was a successful business man and had his stuff together. He was a family man who was focused on his goals. Did you catch, "IT" the key word here is he was focused on HIS goals. Carmel was so caught up with being successful that it was all about him to a fault. Don't get me wrong he was a sweet and caring guy but he was his main priority. He treated Sweetie well and made her feel special. Sweetie understood that he was first in his life and that was the way it was going to be. They tried talking it out and he really wanted to do and be better. But it wasn't long before he reverted to his former way. So instead of staying on a sinking ship Sweetie decided to leave this wonderful guy.

No longer was second best good enough Sweetie could have stayed with Carmel and settled for less than being first in his life. She probably would have lived a nice life, however a nice life was never an option for Sweetie she knew her worth and realized that if she wanted better she would have to change things. Sweetie did not want to risk staying on a ship that had potential. Ladies we have to stop looking at a man's potential and see them for who they are right now. This is not a fairy tale and the happy endings may never come. So be a realist, this is who he is now. When a man really loves you they put you first. So she had to make some severe changes and one was to leave Carmel. Leaving was hard because they were more than on a ship together, they were friends. He was a great guy which made it harder for her to leave. He didn't have to be a jerk he just was not Mr. Right and Sweetie was not being fulfilled in the relationship. She wasn't ready to compromise because he measured up to most of the requirements she had for a man. He was lacking in a major area to Sweetie, one that she could no longer overlook. Carmel was so caught up with his plans that he would sometimes forget what she was working on. When a man loves you he is interested in your dreams. She, like most women, knew his plans for the next five or more years so she could help him achieve them. It is always good to support your man but not to the point you are losing your dreams. There should be room for his dreams and your dream. The man who is perfect for your life will know how to intertwine both yours and his to accomplish the unified goal. Sweetie knew this was a major deal breaker. He was just not Mr. Right so she broke it off and started on her journey to Singletude.

Of course many times on her journey it could have been so easy to go back to Carmel when things got rough or she felt lonely but she didn't. Remember, he was and is a great guy. However, she had fixed in her mind that she was moving forward because good just wasn't good enough. She had focused herself on changing her life for the better. She wanted it all! In order for her to get what she wanted it would require her to make some sacrifices.

If all that another person has to offer is not everything that you require you have to be willing to let them go. Too many times women feel that they can change a man. You can Not! The only person you can change is yourself. Stop falling in love with the man he can become and realize the man he is now. This is who he is, he is not his potential. Yes he has the potential to become so many things but you are not the one who brings out his potential. He is! Nothing you do will make his potential change. If he wants you bad enough he will change. Are you willing to gamble on the fifty/fifty chance that he could? This is your life and you only get one. You do not get to the end with a possibility of a do over. NO! Wasting years on a possibility of potential is not good enough.

Sweetie decided she needed to work on some areas in her own life. You see its fine when we can find fault in other people. The fast track to change is to find what faults lay inside of you. That is when true healing and change can take place. Sweetie started working on foundational stuff in her own life. She knew there was baggage that needed to be opened and handled. Turns out she had some issues that seemed really small when she packed them away. But once she opened up the bag years later and let the issues out she saw how big they really were.

Instead of dealing with the disappointments or break-ups in her life it was easy to just pack them away and move on to the next relationship. Regardless of the cause, the wounds created by these events have to be dealt with or else left alone they will fester from the inside out. You need time to heal and regain your composure and trust before the very issue or hurt you wanted to pack away comes back to sabotage your current and future relationships.

So off she went on her road to Singletude where she found that being single was enjoyable and it could be fun and rewarding. Sweetie was shocked when she found things like joy, happiness and contentment on her road to Singletude. You can enjoy those things too it is yours for the taking. Singleness is not a curse, it is an empowering self-discovery and a time to enjoy the temporary state you are in. Trust me and I say this with conviction, you will not be single forever. Your Mr. Right is alive and breathing and praying for you. Until you learn to enjoy your singleness you will never be able to share in unity with Mr. Right. It is a PROCESS! It is not a punishment it is merely one of the many stages our lives will take over a course of a lifetime. Enjoy where you are, it can be fun. The bible hits this fact directly on the head correctly when saying, "I have learned to be content in whatever state I am in." (Phil 4:12) This should be your banner whether single, married, divorced or widowed. How you view any situation or stage of life will dictate your outcome.

This is not an overnight thing it is a PROCESS! The in-between business is what you are going to have to incorporate into your life. Your success or failure will depend on your ability to follow the triple A's

Assess the situations in your life

Look at the situations for what they truly are, temporary. If you regroup and think it through you will find your way out. If you can't come up with the answers seek out others and be honest with your goals. Don't be the way I was and allow the situation to consume your every thought. It's not that Deep! (INTD) It wasn't until I was able to look at my situation from a Victor's point of view that the answers started to flow on how this thing would turn around. When I did what the bible said and counted it all joy. "Count it all joy my brother when you meet trials of various kinds." (James 1:2) I looked at what was going good in my life and reminded myself how even in this situation I was still blessed.

Assume responsibility for your role

There comes a time when you have to take the big girl pill and realize that some of the things that are happening in your life were brought on by you. Yes I was an active participant in the game of life and my decisions brought me to this point. However, Glory to God I don't have to stay here. I could make the decision to learn from my mistakes. I could learn from the failures of my past so I would not repeat it again. Then I could move on.

Acknowledge that I need God

It wasn't until I allowed God into my whole life that change could begin. You see change is not an action it is a person, Jesus! I told ya'll I accepted him but he was only my Hoe on the side. I don't think God will stand by while we make him our Hoe on the side. He will not force his will on us but you will face consequences for your actions when you step out of God's will for your life. If you are not in his will then in whose are you? You need him! I did and my life has never been the same.

Take the new road and create for you a different way of doing things it's called Change! Your new route can lead you to places that you have not even imagined and on the new route your perfect mate is there waiting for you. Can you just imagine with me for a moment. The day you decide to do things differently and chart out a different course. You begin the process to Singletude and as you take back all the things that were lost, deal with some inner trials and begin to expose the diamond within guess who will definitely show up Mr. Right. It is a fact that we attract the very thing we are looking for when we stop pursuing it and start pursuing God.

LAWS OF SINGLETUDE

The laws of Singletude

1. You have to love and respect yourself
    - If you don't love YOU how can anyone else. It is important to have a healthy self-esteem. Once you can love yourself it will be easy for others to be drawn into that love affair.
2. Remember to enjoy life now
    - If you do not know how to have fun without a significant other, how will you be able to bring a healthy lifestyle to the relationship? It is not the other person's job to make you happy. You have to know how to enjoy your life and what things you like doing. Treat yourself to a massage and buy yourself perfume because it smells good, not because you are trying to entice someone.
3. Find new ways to improve you
    - If there is an area you desire in your mate please make sure that area in you is tight. If you want a man with a beautiful body. Please work towards making yours beautiful. If he has to have straight white teeth a trip to the dentist might be a good idea. If his credit score has to be on point. When was the last time you checked yours. If you want him to own his own business, start working on your business plan.

Improve YOU so you will attract what you want. Nothing looks better to a man than a woman who has a likeness to himself!

4. Clean up
   - Order is key...get your life in order I pray this book has given you a start to the process. Now it is time to take action and use what you have learned. Remember "YOU CAN DO IT!!!!!" Start somewhere, maybe by physically cleaning out your clothing closet will help you to mentally clean out your mental closet. Get started today.

5. Get a plan
   - Write down what you want your life to look like. The bible says write the vision and make it plain. Well the same goes for your life. If you fail to plan you plan to fail. It's not deep you can change and alter it as much as you like. But how will you know where you want your life to go if you don't have a road map of where you are going.

6. Check your surroundings
   - Now that you have decided to live your life in Singledom, with your new Singletude you should surround yourself with people committed to doing the same. If you want to live successfully in any area get around people who have shown through time and patience that they are living their lives well in that

area. Find out how they are getting success in their lives. Be open to thought patterns that are different than yours. Ask them to mentor you and keep you accountable.

SINGLETUDE CONFESSION

Father God, I decree and declare that my single life will glorify you. I receive you as Lord over my body, spirit and soul. I will seek you first in all that I do. I pray that your will fulfill its purpose in my life.
Father God I confess that every financial need is met and that I will not lack or want for anything, In the Name of Jesus. I speak with power and authority that my life is prosperous.
I bind up every generational curse, strongman and stronghold sent against me. I loose the Spirit of Truth, Love, Joy, Peace and Liberty over my Singleness,
In my singleness I will walk in Excellence, Love, Character and Integrity at all times. I will Pray, Fast and do what the word of God says for my life to accomplish what God has set it forth to do with diligence. I place a demand on myself to walk in obedience and submission.
I choose to live a holy life pleasing until God and the lust of my flesh has no power over me. I am committed to be diligent in the things of God. I will spend quality time helping to advance the Kingdom of God,
I thank you in advance for what is going to take place through my life. I receive that it is in your word that when I first Seek the kingdom of God and all its righteousness all things that God has intended for my life shall be added unto me.
Satan you are defeated, I am more than a conqueror in Christ Jesus, and no weapon that is formed against me will prosper. In the name of Jesus I release every ministering Angel assigned to my life to go forth and cause this confession to come to pass.
In Jesus Name Amen.

SALVATION

I contribute all my success to surrendering my life to Christ and accepting him as my Savior.

I could not write a book that does not allow a person the opportunity to accept Jesus for their self. So I am taking this opportunity to do just that offer Salvation to you.

The coolest thing about it is you can do it right from where you are.

Yup, right by yourself and right now if you want to.

Just repeat these words and mean them.

Father God, I come to you in the name of Jesus Christ your son.

In Romans 10:13 it says, "...that whosoever shall call upon the name of the Lord shall be saved.

Father, I am calling on Jesus right now.

I believe He died on the cross for my sin and that He was raised on the third day,

and He's alive right now.

Lord Jesus I'm asking You now, come into my heart.

Live in me and through me.

I repent of my sins and surrender myself totally and completely to You.

Heavenly Father, by faith I now confess Jesus Christ as Lord and from this day forward

I will dedicate my life to serving him

TO REPENT

Just in case you were like me and really didn't know what to repent means. I really thought it was to feel real bad and say that you weren't going to do what you did again. Even thought I didn't really mean it. Well that is not what repentance means. So here is my understanding of it.

The act of true repentance is changing one's mind.. Is it that simple you say? Yes basically. Let me first tell you what it is not.
What to repent does not mean
- It is not a gloomy despair or a feeling of degradation
- It is not quitting a sin for a season
- It is not knowing a action is wrong and feeling bad, and hiding it

What to repent really means
- To totally turn away from that act all together

That's it! I know you thought I had more for you but I don't....it's to turn away from the sin totally and completely. I didn't say to stop the sin I said turn away which means you have to turn to something or hopefully someone..Jesus and ask for his help in dealing with this. He will help you.

The bible even instructs us in I John 1:9 to confess our sins to Him and receive the love of and the forgiveness of God. We also have to spend time in His word so it will help us renew our mind (change our thinking)

Last thing that is helpful when repenting is to go to someone who can be trusted and are mature in the faith and tell them what you are struggling with so that they can be agreement through prayer/fasting and accountability (James 5:16). Remember, you don't have to do this alone. There are people at your church which can go deeper into the meaning of repentance but this is the basics.

SINGLETUDE TERMS

Term	Definition
Singletude	The empowerment to prosper while being saved and single
Despera-tude	The negative attitude about being saved and single
Lonely-tude	State of loneliness towards your current state of singleness
Lost-a-tude	Clueless on what to do, how to do it and where to go about your situation; Lost
Singledom	A place of total peace with yourself about your Singletude
Victim Syndrome	Events done to you, that are over, that you allow to continue to enslave you
Jawn	Not your main partner; derogatory title for someone you don't respect
Hoe	Person you don't care about that you use when you want to, then forget about
Diamonds	How valuable we are to God: womanly essence
INTD	It's not that deep
Prayer Life	Time set aside for prayer that is a part of your daily life
Read your bible	A set time each day that you read the bible

Term	Definition
Time with God	Worship time spent daily with God
Power	The ability to depend on God
Pride	Your puffed up vision of who you are not who God says you are
Success	What you work at daily to achieve
Faith	The substance of things hoped for evidence of things not seen (Heb 11:1)
Truth	Word of God
Force	The backing of the word of God active in your life
Goals	Written plan for your life with the desired results
Ecstasy	Overwhelming feeling of great happiness or joyful excitement
Destiny	The end result of who God created you to become
Sexified	Satisfied only sexually
Penagina trap	A trap set when you allow your penis or vagina to make decisions

SINGLETUDE-JOURNAL

CONTENTS

18. Introduction to Journal

19. Your Story

20. New Life in Singleness

21. Information is the Key to Breakthrough

22. Wrong Thinking

23. To have sex or not to have sex

24. I am not built for this

25. E-Factor

26. Diamonds

27. Don't Quit

INTRODUCTION

This journal was designed so that while you are on journey to Singletude you can track yourself along the way. I want you to use this journal as a roadmap along the way. Make it an interactive activity while reading.

Read

This is the easy part you get to read and enjoy Singletude the book. While you're reading when something grabs you or gives you an, "Ah Ha" moment write a short note to yourself and proceed. Not everything will apply but there will be keys along the way that will help unlock some challenges in your life write it down. Finally if this chapter was really good to you and you would like to tell me about email me if you know a friend who could really use this write it down so you can tell them. I have listed some step by step things that may assist you in your journey pack them in your travel bag and bring them along for the trip.

Reflect

This is where you get to share your thoughts on the subject. I want you to do this so you will be able to know how you were thinking in the beginning and when you reach your destination you will know some of your challenges and triumphs that helped to get you there. We cannot proceed into our future without resolving our past. This journal can be an important piece of the process. Be honest with yourself this is your book no one else has to read it. I wish this existed when I was on my journey to Singletude. It would have made such a big difference.

Rethink

Relax, and understand that Rome wasn't built in a day and your journal should be completed one day at a time. This is not a marathon that has a time limit for completion. It is your pace but I promise you one thing once you make the decisions to change your circumstances and live in Singledom you will feel like you're on a fast track to success. Learn to enjoy life during the process.
There will be tips that are from the book and others that are solely for this journal all geared toward you achieving success while single.

YOUR STORY

You have just read the story of my life, well a portion of my life but it was the determining factor. It was when things started to turn around. Use this part of the book to write a story about yourself and define what will be your determining factor on your road to Singletude.

List the scripture from the bible you will use to associate with while on your journey.

_____
_____

Tell your story. You can edit later just write about you and your life triumphs, defeats and your determining factor. Get started.....

_____
_____
_____
_____
_____
_____
_____

_____
_____
_____
_____
_____
_____
_____
_____
_____
_____
_____
_____
_____
_____
_____
_____
_____
_____
_____
_____
_____
_____

Forgiveness

    The greatest thing I learned about Forgiving is that it is not for them. It releases you. You know what is strange about unforgiveness the people you refuse to forgive don't even think about the situation/event that hurt you. You're not talking to them are being nasty to them or planning revenge is not even on their mind. Most of the time they have moved on from that situation you are the one who can't get past it. It's eating you alive from the inside out causing you pain and heartache. Stop it, Forgive them, I know your saying but you don't know what they did to me. I don't care the only way to move past the hurt is to forgive. Your gonna have to trust me on some things and by the end of the book you will get it OK! FORGIVE!!!!! (Ch 1.)

Now that you have it written down give it to God! Forgive yourself and others. Remember forgiveness is for you.

Notes:
_____
_____
_____

Ah Ha moment:
_____
_____
_____
_____
_____
_____

List the top things that you plan to give to God:
_____
_____
_____
_____

"You only live once but if you do it right once is enough" Mae West

NEW LIFE IN SINGLENESS

My spirit was brand new but everything else remained the same. I still was as mean as I was before I was saved. This is the beginning of the rest of your life. You have the opportunity right now to CHOOSE how it will go.

_____
_____
_____
_____
_____
_____
_____
_____
_____
_____

Make this the start of something good for you.

Write out what your new life will look like. Here are a few practical steps you can use.

1. Find out what you are seeking God for? (if you're not seeking him than get started)
2. What have you done about it?

3. Where are you spiritually?
4. List the things that will be unacceptable in your life from this point forward
5. Get some goals for your all the areas of your life (Spiritual, Work, Family, etc)

You are going to have to be an active participant in your life. Gone are the days of using Jesus as your Hoe, you are going to have to be in relationship with him for real. That means spending time learning about him.

- You learn by listening to others who know him
- Reading your bible
- Spending time with him

I suggest joining a church who studies the word of God and really studying in your private time. It is the only way. The Bible says He will direct your path……. You can find that out and all sorts of wonderful other things that is in there. For those of you who already know this all I can say is…… Trust him!

Get a Singletude life book (I have one) in this book I want you to place all the things you will believe God for and what you are willing to work continuously toward.

- Map out your life with pictures and words
    - Look in magazines and find the things you want to accomplish and cut the pictures out. I have heard that a picture is worth a thousand words so get some. These pictures will remind you what you are working so when it

gets hard and it may you can see them and be inspired to continue.
- Do a timeline
    - I want you to block your goals out. We will call this our life map with pictures. First find the things you want to accomplish in all the areas we discussed earlier. Then figure out what year you would like for it to happen. Then what needs to be done in order to complete the goal.
        - Example: Goal – Get out of debt in five years
        - Find out debt – Get help with a professional
        - Decide what you can pay monthly
        - Where you should be by end of this year, 1st qtr of the next year, midyear and at the end of year two till you get to five years
        - Get started
    - This is what you are going to have to do for each area. It is your map to help you measure how you are doing. How will you know where you are if there is nothing to measure it by?

- Make it cute
  - It should look like something you enjoy looking at your favorite color, style you know something you cherish. You can even get a group of your friends over with a stack of magazines and have a Life book party!
- Do it!!!!!
  - After you have had the party and figured out where you are going with your new found Singleness. This is the important part start doing it. You are more than capable of completing these things, before you know it you will have to start a new book because you have accomplished everything. Remember we can do all things through Christ that gives us strength.

"Insanity is doing the same thing expecting a different result,"
Ben Franklin

INFORMATION IS THE KEY TO BREAKTHROUGH

I was determined to find out all the information I could. I needed this for my survival. Information is the key to the breakthrough! In order for your life to change you are going to have to change your thinking. How you change your thinking is by getting new information put in to replace the old information. This starts with the word of God but it does not stop there. If there is an area in your life that need fixing, find someone who has fixed theirs and ask them questions. Take classes, go to seminars, and read books on the subject. Do whatever it takes to find the answers to your questions. This is the reason I wrote this book I needed answers so I started asking people who were living successful in the area I was struggling with. It made the difference. You can use this in your Singletude, in your finances, your business whatever. It is the same concept for everything there is no need to re-invent the wheel it already exists. No need to make it up find someone who has conquered your issue and talk to them they love to talk about it, I know I enjoy it and can't wait for any opportunity to assist someone.

What am I trying to fix:

Who do I know in my life that displays this:

What if any conferences are going on this year I can attend:

"Spend time with the wise and you will become wise,
but friends of fools will suffer,
Proverbs 13:20

WRONG THINKING

Wrong Thinking – Control your thoughts and keep them pure and of good nature. If you find your mind is going into places that you are trying to correct find a person to be accountable to. This is so important you need help, now that you have asked God for help allow him to lead you to people that can assist.

Who do I know that I can be honest with and they will keep it confidential?

_____
_____
_____
_____
_____

When do I notice that my mind goes back to old thoughts and what I am doing when this happen

_____
_____
_____
_____
_____

What are my plans when these thought come back up?

_____
_____
_____
_____
_____

You have a responsibility to yourself to protect what you are building. That includes protection from the old you. The bible says your word have I hid in my heart that I might not sin against you. I am convinced the closer you get to God the more old things and thoughts will start to change.

They say you can't fight a thought with a thought, so pick a scripture for the areas you are trying to change. When that old way of thinking comes up remind yourself with the words of God first and then remember why you are working on that area.

_____
_____
_____
_____
_____
_____

"Change does not roll in on the wheels of inevitability, but comes through continuous struggle," Martin Luther King

TO HAVE SEX OR NOT TO HAVE SEX

I don't just want sexual fulfillment, I want it all! I want and require a loving respectful relationship that will lead to marriage. The only way to get it is learn how to make the hard decisions. I really want it all, and the only way to get it is to continue to maintain who I am despite my emotion. The verse I was reminded of, "But seek ye first the kingdom of God, and his righteousness; and all these things shall be added unto you."

Like I told you in this chapter I am not immune to wanting to enjoy the release of sexual satisfaction, however I want it in the confines of marriage. That is the only way the Bible explains that it is permissible. Look even God said it is not good for man to be alone, so I am not telling you to be alone for the rest of your life. I am saying if you are tired of what you have been experiencing and you are ready to really enjoy what it means to have sex. Do it His way.

He created Sex in marriage for you to enjoy how much more enjoyable will it be when it carries no negative emotions with it. I believe the two becoming one means something that even physical satisfaction can't compare to its pleasure. When Sex in done the way it was intended I know there are levels of satisfaction that we

just can't conceive until we are doing it properly. Wow!!!! That's right I am saying this, "there is levels of satisfaction you can't even imagine and you can have it. Don't settle for anything but God's best and then enjoy! His word says, "Delight yourself in the Lord and he will give you the desires of your heart!" Psalms 37:4
What is it that you desire?

_____

_____

_____

_____

_____

_____

_____

_____

The things I plan on fixing about me before my mate gets here:

_____

_____

_____

_____

_____

_____

I told you guys how I prayed to God to send my husband so I would not sin…..Well if he would have sent him then I would have jacked him up. To put it quite honestly the only thing I was ready for was sex. Not the precious gift that will be given to me. I would have caused us all kinds of heartache. I know it, if you are true to yourself think about your life right now and what would happen if God blessed you right now. Please be honest! Think long and hard most of yall would agree you are not ready. So let's continue to get moving toward Singletude and get ready so when he shows up you are at a good place in your life. Then you both can truly enjoy each other and lots of SEX!!!!! You are more than capable of doing it!

"All great accomplishments require time" Maya Angelou

I AM NOT BUILT FOR THIS

You are definitely built for this and more. The bible says we were fearfully and wonderfully made. Which means we are capable of doing exactly as it, "the Bible" is instructing you. You were never meant for some of the relationships you got into. You were never meant to experience some of the people you have experienced. You were built for better and greater things.

I understand that society and some people in the church have decided to give its spin on how things should go within a relationship. If you are TRULY going to get to Singletude you are going to have to follow the blue print sent before us. The Bible is the manual for our lives and that is what our point of reference should only be.

_____
_____
_____
_____
_____
_____
_____

I have tried it my way and failed over and over again. It wasn't until I started doing things the way the Bible instructs me when I started experiencing Victory in every area of my life. I tell you as a living witness that it works. I didn't like it and I am not asking you to like it I am asking you to trust and do it. When your life starts changing for the better you will like it.

List the top five reasons you think you are not built for this:

_____

_____

_____

_____

_____

Go back and read the story of how tough you were built and how God sees you. You are more than a conqueror through Christ. Just have Faith and trust in him.

"Charm is deceptive, and beauty is fleeting; but a woman who fears the Lord is to be praised,"
Proverbs 31:30

E-FACTOR

The E-factor is not instant so you will not fall prey to catching and falling in love with the wrong guy if you use the other great thing God has given us....YOUR BRAINS, I have often heard the term when someone shows you or tells you who they are BELIEVE THEM. Ladies we have been created with the ability to love and love deeply make sure that the person you are lining up for that type of love is worth it.

Write a time when you fell for the E-factor:

_____
_____
_____
_____
_____

Now that you are aware of the E-factor what do you plan to do to protect yourself from the negative side of it.

_____
_____
_____
_____
_____

The E-factor in itself it not a negative thing, it's when because of whatever reason we allow someone to pursue us after our instincts have told us he is not the one. Our instincts and intuitions are given to help guide us along in life. Stop over ruling the connectors that God has placed inside of you. They were put there for a reason. Stop believing the potential of a man. He is who he is! If you think there is greatness in him, it is not your job to figure it out. It is his, so allow him the time to get it together and while he's doing his thing you get your thing in order!

Trust your instincts in the beginning and do not be persuaded by his looks or his attention. This is what I have come up to assist me with accomplishing it.

"When someone shows you who they are, believe them the first time" Oprah Winfrey

DIAMONDS

I asked Benefitisha what she would do if I gave her a handful of rare diamonds. Would she just give them away to anyone who asked? Her answer was a roaring, "NO!!!" She said she would not give them to anyone. She would keep these rare and expensive jewels to herself. Well Houston! We have a problem!!!! God views us as rare and of immeasurable quality. He calls our bodies' temples of the Holy Spirit.

Diamonds are classified by ratings the rarer it is, the more value it is worth. That is how we as women should think of our bodies. You are special....Let me say it again...YOU ARE SPECIAL! If no one else sees you that way always remember Elohim, the King of kings calls you special. So special that he has inspired pages of whom you are in him. "She is worth far more than rubies...a woman who fears the Lord is to be praised." (Prov. 31) This is how your creator sees you as a woman of worth and value. You are not just a sex buddy.

Notes to self:

_____

_____

_____

"...We are the change we seek." President Barack Obama

DON'T QUIT

What is it going to take!

There sometimes is a serious disconnect between what we want and what it really is going to take to achieve it. Everyone knows the saying, "if you want something different you have to do something different." Writing this book has been my way of showing you that this concept really works. I can write about Singletude because I experience it every day. However, It did not come without challenges....I had many, but the defining factor was when I decided that I can't have something new doing old things. That was when things started to turn around for me. I want the same success that I achieved for you.

Write down the things you are going to say goodbye to in order to embrace the things you want.

_____
_____
_____
_____
_____
_____
_____

While it is easy to go from point A to point B when writing and a person could miss the in between's. Believe me this is not an overnight thing it is a PROCESS! The in-between business is what you are going to have to incorporate into your life. Your success or failure will depend on your ability to do the 3 A's, Assess, Assume and Acknowledge.

Assess the situations in your life

Look at the situations for what they truly are, temporary. If you regroup and think it through you will find your way out. If you can't come up with the answers seek out others and be honest with your goals. Don't be the way I was and allow the situation to consume your every thought. It's not that Deep! (INTD) It wasn't until I was able to look at my situation from a Victor's point of view that the answers started to flow on how this thing would turn around. When I did what the bible said, "Count it all joy my brother when you meet trials of various kinds." (James 1:2) I looked at what was going good in my life and reminded myself how even in this situation I was still blessed.

Assume responsibility for your role

There comes a time when you have to take the big girl pill and realize that some of the things that are happening in your life were brought on by you. I was an active participant in the game of life and my decisions brought me to this point. However, Glory to God I didn't have to stay here. I could make the decision to learn from my mistakes. I could learn from the failures of my past so I would not repeat it again. Then I could move on.

Acknowledge that I need God

It wasn't until I allowed God into my whole life that change could begin. You see change is not an action it is a person, Jesus! I told ya'll I accepted him but he was only my Hoe on the side. He will not force his will on us but you will face consequences for your actions when you step out of God's will for your life. If you are not in his will, then in whose are you? You need him! I did and my life has never been the same.

Take the new route created for you a different way of doing things it's called Change! Your new route can lead you to places that you have not even imagined. On the new route your perfect mate is there waiting for you. Can you just imagine with me for a moment. The day you decide to do things differently and chart out a different course. You begin the process to Singletude and as you take back all the things that were lost, deal with some inner trials and begin to expose the diamond within guess who will definitely show up Mr. Right. It is a fact that we attract the very thing we are looking for when we stop pursuing it and start pursuing God!

"You can do whatever you put your mind to" Ruth Copes
(Thanks Momma you were right!)

ACKNOWLEDGMENTS

I would like to thank my editor Fairley Hopkins who kept telling me there is a lot of people who need to read this book. A special thanks to Christopher "Chris D" Daniels for walking me through the process. To all my family and friends who prayed for me, encouraged me, and kept asking when it would be finished. Here it is! Enjoy.

Unless otherwise identified, all Scripture quotations in this book are from the New International Version of the Bible.

Cover Photo:
> Femqua Productions
> Porsha Antalan
> 912-980-3964 912-980-3964
> http://www.femqua.com

Model on cover (my niece auntie loves you):
> Tierra Benton
> 678-343-5080
> Tierra.benton1@gmail.com

Photo on back:
> Chris Engel Photography
> www.Chrisengelphotography.blogspot.com
> www.indonesiagirl09@yahoo.com

Contact info:
> Singletude@yahoo.om
> Twitter.com/S1NGLETUDE
> https://www.facebook.com/Singletude

Made in the
USA
Monee, IL